Changing Relationships:
Shared Action Planning with
People with a Mental Handicap

This book was originally written and published in 1986 as a component of the Open University course P555, 'Mental Handicap: Patterns for Living'. Minor modifications have been made to the text so that it can be read and used independently from the rest of the course.

The course itself was prepared in collaboration with MENCAP for people who are involved with children or adults with mental handicap; that includes many people from different backgrounds, such as parents and staff, professionals and volunteers, in a variety of residential, day and community settings. The course is part of the Open University's programme of Continuing Education, and can be studied by people either working on their own in their own time or as a member of a group, sharing thoughts and experiences with others. There are four main texts for the course. Different viewpoints and experiences are presented through real-life accounts from individuals, their families and the various staff and volunteers involved with them. The course books are:

- Book One: *Living and Learning*
- Book Two: *Changes and Choices*
- Book Three: *Support Networks and Resources*
- Book Four: *Strategies for Change*

Along with other resources including this skills workbook, the course pack contains four audio-cassette programmes and a media booklet. There are also four TV programmes associated with the course.

The course aims to support people who are involved in the changes taking place in the lives of people with mental handicap, and who want to help to make these changes positive.

The course is available to anybody who wishes to purchase a pack of the materials. If you would like further information about the course write to:

Jenny Rook
Information Officer
Department of Health and Social Welfare
North Spur Building
The Open University
Milton Keynes
MK7 6AA

Changing Relationships: Shared Action Planning with People with a Mental Handicap

ANN BRECHIN

*Lecturer in Health & Social Welfare,
The Open University*

and

JOHN SWAIN

*Lecturer in Special Educational Needs,
Newcastle Polytechnic*

Harper & Row, Publishers
London

Cambridge
Mexico City
New York
Philadelphia

San Francisco
São Paulo
Singapore
Sydney

ILTK

B

First published 1986, this edition published 1987

Harper & Row Ltd
28 Tavistock Street
London WC2E 7PN

British Library Cataloguing in Publication Data
Brechin, Ann
    Changing relationships: shared action planning with people with a mental
    handicap.
    1. Mentally handicapped—Means of communication
    2. Interpersonal relations
    3. Social work with the mentally handicapped
    I. Title   II. Swain, John
    362.2'042   HV3004.5

    ISBN 0-06-318394-3

Typeset by Burns & Smith, Derby
Printed and bound by Butler & Tanner Ltd, Frome and London

CONTENTS

PREFACE

Relationships are changing. Many more people with the label of mental handicap are beginning to express their own wishes and make their own decisions about what their futures hold. Parents and professionals in turn have to learn how to respond to the different role that is now demanded of them. New relationships have to develop which involve a more equal partnership. None of this is particularly easy, but if such statements are to be more than just lip-service, then new approaches have to be developed which can support this process of emancipation.

What is offered in this book is a revised approach to Individual Programme Planning; an approach intended to support those people most closely involved in 'changing relationships'.

Individual Programme Planning provided a valuable impetus towards some of the changes which are now occurring. Its crucial message has been that planning for individuals in the light of their strengths, needs and particular circumstances is a great deal more satisfactory than the blanket provisions which tend to occur routinely. Increasingly though, with the growth of self-advocacy and the greater possibilities for independence and self-determination to be found in community-based living, Individual Programme Planning no longer adequately fits the bill. Relationships have moved on and outgrown some of the original assumptions.

Many people are involved in these changes; parents, care staff, day-centre workers, nurses, other professionals, and people with learning difficulties themselves. In developing the concept of Shared Action Planning, we have tried to find an approach which draws on people's existing skills and understanding of personal relationships and builds from there. Professional expertise is seen in this context as one rather specialized way of approaching processes we are all involved in. Partnerships can be encouraged when people begin to understand the similarities between each other's behaviour, rather than concentrating on the differences.

Behind the ideas in Shared Action Planning is a commitment to those people who usually have least opportunity to develop and express their views about what should happen next: people such as parents or unqualified staff, who may be closely involved but lack the power or information to make key decisions; and people with learning difficulties themselves, who may these days be 'consulted', but lack the time or opportunity to develop their ideas properly. In this sense this book is about the skills of communication, about listening to people, and about people developing and thinking through their own ideas, as in self-advocacy. It is about sharing and gaining confidence, and it is about the growth and change of relationships as that confidence emerges.

Developing ideas, however, is only a part of the process, and the essential 'Action Planning' concentrates on the kinds of possibilities that exist for action. What might people actually do differently? In this context the book is also about how people learn new skills, how people's behaviour can change, how opportunities can be developed, and what encourages or makes possible any new developments. Another key difference in the Shared Action Planning approach is a shift away from the emphasis on making people with mental handicap change – from what they can do now, to what they ought to do next. This is often what tends to come out of Individual Programme Planning. The emphasis here has been broadened. Maybe other people need to change their behaviour; maybe other opportunities need to be created.

We offer you the approach we have called Shared Action Planning in the hope that it can help to create some of those 'other opportunities' within new partnerships. We hope you will find that Shared Action Planning can play an important role for you as part of a continuing process of changing relationships.

Ann Brechin
John Swain
April 1987

ACKNOWLEDGEMENTS

Our thanks go to the many people who contributed their thoughts and ideas as this book was developed and whose critical reading of our early drafts forced us to think even harder about our ideas: to Dorothy Atkinson, Linda Ward, Mary Holland and Jan Walmsley, who faced the challenge with us as members of the original course team; to Roger Blunden, Mary John, Professor Malcolm Johnson, Professor Chris Kiernan, Alan Parrish, Professor Oliver Russell, Pam Shakespeare, Alan Tyne, Paul Williams and Ray Woolfe, who found the time somehow to read and comment helpfully on successive drafts; to Peter Righton who was a soul mate in the early stages of struggling with the tangled web of half-formed ideas.

We thank Christine Love for her endless days of patient typing and retyping – and for not minding! We thank Colin Wheeler for turning our ideas into wonderful cartoons; Keith Howard for bringing people to life with his drawings; Rich Hoyle as graphic designer and Peter Lee as editor for making the original Open University publication just as good as it could be; and Griselda Campbell, our editor with Harper & Row, for steering us on a simple and trouble-free course to this publication.

In particular we thank those who helped to test out the material: Pam Ayers, Chris Cullen, Colin Dale, Liz and Paul Eagle, Norma Graham, Willie Gray, Dick Jones, Marion Lever, Terry Mooney, Maureen Nuttall, Dave Savage, Terry Scragg, Anne Tombs, Margaret Todd, Jean Willson, Adrienne Woolfe, Peter Woods, Marie Woods, and the many other individuals who worked through the material and commented helpfully.

Their thoughtful contributions, many of which have been incorporated, will be appreciated by all who read this book.

Finally our grateful thanks go to our own families: Jade, Anna, Daniel, Samuel and Tamsin in Newcastle; and Derek, Emily, Lucy and Tessa in Milton Keynes, without whose patience and encouragement none of this could have been achieved.

The Posy Simmonds cartoon on page 101 is reproduced by permission of A. D. Peters and Co. Ltd. Copyright © Posy Simmonds.

INTRODUCTION:
HOW TO USE THIS BOOK

A number of features and techniques have been included in the design of this book to help you to study, evaluate, adapt and use a Shared Action Planning approach.

- It has been designed as a skills workbook. There are specific activities to do giving you opportunities to respond to the ideas being presented. There are also Shared Action Planning activities which take you step-by-step through the forms as you work together with a partner with mental handicap. In general this is a book to 'answer back' as you go along, making notes and keeping a record of your progress. We suggest that you keep all your notes in one place and start a Shared Action Planning notebook, ringbinder or file.
- The 'Forms and Guidelines' Appendix provides a summary of the Shared Action Planning approach with sample forms, to be read and used in the first instance in conjunction with the workbook as a whole. You may need to adapt the forms to suit the circumstances and purposes of yourself and the person with whom you are doing the planning.
- This workbook was read, worked through and commented on in draft form by a wide range of people, including parents, people with mental handicap, hostel staff, adult training-centre staff, nurses and nursing assistants, social workers, community nurses, health visitors and volunteers. You will meet some of their comments as you progress through the workbook.
- Throughout the workbook, in boxes, you will find specific accounts

and examples often using the actual words of the people involved. They are there to highlight and illustrate some of the points being made in the text.

● We have also included 'information sections' which give further detailed information about approaches and ideas being discussed in the text.

It is a book to work through, rather than a book to read, and it has been designed carefully to help you to get the most out of the new ideas in it. We hope that you will enjoy the experience.

CHAPTER 1
RELATIONSHIPS:
THE HEART OF THE MATTER

IMPROVING SKILLS

Let us start from where you are: you are already a skilled person. The skills discussed and explored in this book are not just for 'experts', though many professionals would see them as crucial to their work. These skills are part and parcel of day-to-day living. They are used in friendships, family living, relationships at work and in mutual helping and caring. Such skills grow and develop through and within personal relationships. Relationships are, in this sense, the heart of the matter.

So, as we said, you already have skills and the workbook starts from where you are. It is designed to help you to build on your own ideas and experiences by trying out in your own life or work setting the approach suggested here. The overall aim is not to offer specific answers. As one of the people involved in assessing this approach said: 'Blanket rules should not apply'. The aim is to look for ways and means of finding answers:

- ways which you and the people in your life can use to find answers together
- answers which feel right to you and which can work for you in your particular situation.

In a skills workbook, the focus must be on skills. According to the *Oxford English Dictionary*, *skill* means:

'expertness, practical ability, facility in an action or in doing or planning to do something'.

But how are skills acquired? How do you learn to ride a bike for example? Reading or hearing explanations might help, but perhaps reading about or watching the experiences of others helps too. Obviously something more has to happen. Acquiring or developing skills always involves building on existing abilities by trying out and practising new approaches.

- People need to build on existing knowledge, experience and skills. On a bike this means drawing on the ability to co-ordinate hands, eyes and feet, and a sense of balance and an understanding of how pedals work, for example.
- People need to have a go; to try out and practise a new approach. How else could anyone discover it really is possible for them to balance on two wheels?

Our concern here, however, is not simply with physical or mechanical skills involving machines. It is about the skills people use in working, learning, living, and being together, and is therefore even more challenging. These skills are the fabric of everyday relationships between people. Examining and developing skills must therefore also mean examining and developing relationships. We need to think about relationships which help us to grow and develop as people. And we need to consider how relationships themselves can be open to growth, development and change.

It is not surprising that many questions tend to arise for people in thinking about the skills involved in such complex processes of 'changing relationships'.

- Questions about yourself: Improving your skills will involve you in thinking through the way you yourself relate to and approach the person or people with whom you live or work. Are you open to change in yourself and your relationships?

- Questions about opportunities: It will also involve you in considering the living circumstances and opportunities in work, leisure and education available to yourself and others.

- Questions about support networks and resources: There are questions, for instance, about the need on the one hand for joining forces with others to share ideas and offer mutual support, and on the other hand, for self-advocacy to enhance the role played by people with mental handicap in developing and speaking out about their own views. The need for support in the process of change includes both organizational support which should be built into the structures in which you work, and personal support which can arise informally in the course of your contact with relatives, friends or colleagues.

- Questions about change: Changes sometimes happen to people whether they want them or not. Even when welcomed and planned for, such processes are seldom simple: there can be losses as well as gains, risks are involved and the need for support is crucial. Change can have ripple effects when one change in a person or a system results in a series of changes in people's lives. People may also find barriers to change which have to be recognized and overcome. Change inevitably involves uncertainties and is likely to raise many questions. Are you willing to take the risk?

- Questions about relationships: 'Who is to change?' one person asked. Now you might be asking, 'Whose skills are we talking about? Your skills or the skills of the people in your life with mental handicap?' We believe the two go hand in hand as a two-way thing. A two-way thing requires a relationship based on equality and mutual benefit. That is the basis of the approach in this workbook. Many of the activities are devised to develop skills through working, talking with and spending time with people with mental handicap. Everyone can be involved together in building on existing skills and developing new ones. 'Skills for People', described in the information section following, is a project which illustrates this nicely.

Skills for People

Skills for People is a project which runs open courses and workshops in Newcastle. Small working groups plan and organize each event achieving an average of one full-day course a week during the project's two-and-a-half year life.

This is not, as you might expect, a project where professionals offer parents some skills-training workshops for them to practise, in turn, on their handicapped children; nor is it a version of a self-advocacy group, with support and skills development offered by professionals to a group of people with mental handicap. This is a project in which people with all kinds of handicap, including mental handicap, work together with parents, relatives, professionals and volunteers to plan and run the courses and workshops.

The aim is to increase people's abilities to work together on an equal basis in their local communities, and to increase the extent to which people with a handicap can make their own decisions and run their own lives.

The project is unique in three ways:

1 It deliberately involves people with a handicap in providing services for themselves. This includes:

- being a small group discussion leader at workshops/courses
- being a member of the Programme Committee; deciding what the programme priorities for the project will be
- being a member of working parties which plan and evaluate services for people with a handicap
- evaluating the services of Skills for People over the last two years

2 The content of Skills for People courses is different from that usually offered. The project covers issues that are rarely dealt with, such as sexuality, and issues which have formerly been discussed mostly by professionals, such as the principles of normalization. Other topics include:

- how to stand up for yourself
- how to be a public speaker
- how groups work and how I work in groups

- how to prepare for your own individual programme plan
- how to write for grants and raise funds
- how to evaluate whether a programme achieves what it sets out to do.

3 Most members of the Speakers' Bureau are people with a handicap and parents or relatives. Their presentations at conferences and training seminars for professionals have had a great deal of impact. Everybody learns from the experience.

Skills for People, Haldane House,
Tankerville Terrace, Jesmond,
Newcastle upon Tyne, NE2 3AH

RELATIONSHIPS: WHAT DO THEY OFFER?

A personal relationship involves an emotional commitment between two people. This can vary from the close and intimate bonds of love to supportive and compassionate working relationships. It may also, of course, be a negative experience. A personal relationship usually involves being together with another person over a long period of time, though of course we can feel closely involved with people we rarely or never see. It can include friendships, marriages, some professional/client relationships, those between parent and child, and between workmates. The more casual contacts with passers-by in the community are not usually thought of as personal relationships, though they can nevertheless have a strong impact and we will return to them later in this workbook.

Few people would deny the general importance of close relationships in their lives. If you have the right kind of relationships with others, you are likely to live longer, to enjoy better physical and mental health, and to feel happier. If you wish, you can look at a book by Argyle and Henderson (1985) for a fuller discussion of this.

Activity

What is it that relationships with other people do for you? Think of an important personal relationship in your life. Write down a list of all the different kinds of benefits you get from the relationship. Then list any benefits that you think the other person gets.

YOUR RELATIONSHIP WITH ....
Benefits for you   Benefits for the other person

This question of what people get from relationships with other people was considered at a conference of people with a mental handicap, parents and residential workers in America. The quotes included below are from the report of that conference ('Personal Relationships for Persons with Developmental Disabilities', 1985).

Knowing who we are
It is through our relationships with others that we learn about ourselves and also, at least partly, become the people we are. 'A person gains confidence as he or she is successful at getting along with others he or she likes.'

Affection and security
Others give us love and emotional security, but they also give us the possibility of loving and feeling needed. 'It's almost as if relationships is a life safety issue.'

Sharing feelings and ideas
We can confide in others and they in us. Close relationships can offer understanding and possibilities for talking about intimate feelings. 'Don't live on lonely street.'

Activities and interests
Personal relationships offer our main social activities, such as companionship, conversation, leisure, play and common interests. 'Put simply, having friends is *fun!*'

Practical help
Practical help refers to all kinds of material and active support people offer each other, including lending money, babysitting, pushing the car and so on. 'Most people get practical help from others who are nearby.'

Advice and information
Other people are a main source of information and advice. 'People learn from each other.'

Relationships are not automatically helpful, however. There are many barriers that can arise: barriers from labelling people as different from other people and from having separate schooling and living arrangements; barriers, too, built into the patterns of our own behaviours. We may

- do things for people when they are capable of doing it for themselves
- not give a person with a mental handicap the opportunities and help they need to make their own choices and decisions
- not listen
- not allow any risks to be taken
- not know what to do for the best

So what kind of relationships *do* promote growth and well-being?

Activity

Think of a relationship that you have with another person which seems to offer you *support and growth*, and ask yourself: what seem to be the important things about the relationship? Make a list of some words or phrases which describe what the relationship is like. This is another question that was discussed at the conference in America mentioned. To help you in your thinking, these are four of the pictures the participants used to illustrate their ideas about different kinds of relationship.

'Like cement.'   'Mutual sharing.'
'Hold things together   'Give and take.'
for people.'
'Hold people together.'

'Being in contact.'   'Proximity.'
'Doing things in harmony.'   'Attachment.'

Ways to describe your supportive relationship

There are many words you might have used. We have put only four main headings to cover a range of possibilities. The following ideas are adapted mainly from the work of Carl Rogers (particularly his book called *Carl Rogers on Personal Power, 1978*).

Genuineness

Genuineness involves the possibility of 'being yourself' in the relationship and the feeling that the other person is genuine. The more that genuine feelings and attitudes can be shared, the more helpful the relationship may be. It's feelings and attitudes that are important when expressed, not opinions and judgements about the other person.

Acceptance

Feelings of self-worth are gained through our relationships with others. If you are accepted as a worthwhile person you are more likely to see yourself positively.

Empathy

Empathy is a shared understanding and sensitivity between two people.

When there is empathy you will feel confident that the other person really understands you.

Warmth

Perhaps you put 'love' at the top of your list? Certainly it is difficult to think of relationships which provide a climate for growth and change without thinking of mutual warmth and satisfaction. Perlman (1979), discussing mainly professional relationships, points out that this does not necessarily imply love. It can mean a positive interest in the other person and a concern for his or her well-being.

Did some of these words – 'genuineness', 'acceptance', 'empathy' and 'warmth' – crop up in your list in some form? The short account of 'Fostering Julie', written by her foster father, shows some of these factors coming into play to encourage Julie's growth and well-being.

Fostering Julie

'We became Julie's foster parents when she was 12 years old. At the time she weighed less than two stone [13 kg]. She was painfully thin, emaciated and without colour. She spat constantly, throwing out a ball of saliva every few seconds – within minutes a pool would be formed at her feet – as she walked she left a trail. In the same unconscious matter-of-fact way, she masturbated. One hand was permanently fiddling between her legs, to the extent that she had worn holes through her clothing. She never ate spontaneously, would never eat sweets like other children, but reacted to food with little short of terror saying that she couldn't eat, that she was handicapped. In a similar way she was terrified of using the toilet, and could retain her faeces with a yogic control. Left to her own devices, Julie would stand with her head bent to the floor – recognizing people by their shoes rather than their faces – and do little other than spit and masturbate.

Julie had not developed the emotional self-sufficiency and independence required for healthy relationships with other people. She totally lacked self-esteem – seeing herself as an unlovable handicapped child with "dirty habits". She sought and expected rejection from other people, yet also used her behaviour problems to ensure her total dependence on others.

She had lived in the care of a local authority from early childhood

(continued)

---

and had been passed from a nursery, to a children's home, to a hostel for mentally handicapped people, to a hospital for mentally handicapped people where we met her. In the hospital she was placed on what is called a "high dependency" ward where she lived with 25 profoundly and multiply handicapped children, none of whom had any real speech, many being immobile, unable to feed themselves or use the toilet.

Through our experiences with Julie, we have come to understand that being a foster parent to such a child requires far more than providing a family life – with all the important details that that entails – eating at the same table with the family, using the same bath, the same toilet as the rest of the family. We found that there were a number of "simple" rules, at least they sounded simple but were very difficult to put into practice. We learnt them the hard way.

1   "Keep a balance between involvement and detachment."
    Julie needed love, not a patronizing or sentimental attitude, but powerful emotions which "demanded" love in return. But we also needed detachment when we were rejected rather than loved in return.
2   "Where possible avoid a crisis."
    We found many ways of changing things (e.g. the position of the table at mealtimes or taking a day-trip to the seaside). It helped relieve the tension.
3   "Never to reject Julie."
    How do you show a child that though what she says or does is "wrong", she herself is accepted and loved? Perhaps it is a matter of time more than anything else.
4   'Persevere."
    Keep going.
5   "Don't expect too much of Julie."
    We learnt to aim at and rejoice in small improvements, e.g. being able to drink from a cup without having to be persuaded to take each swallow.
6   "Keep a diary."
7   "Look for and accept regular relief."
    It was difficult to let others look after Julie, but we needed breaks.
    Perhaps our last "rule" would be "don't believe in golden rules".'

You can read about Julie and her foster family in Swain (1977).

So far in this chapter you have been thinking about:

(a) What people can gain through personal relationships.
(b) The qualities of relationships which can promote growth and well-being (helping people to live and to learn).

We need now to become more concrete, to narrow our focus and look at what actually happens between people when they are together.

THE TWO-WAY COMMUNICATION PROCESS

There is great power in relationships between people. If we think of it as 'power' then it could be said that the electricity of relationships is the *communication*. When feelings, ideas or thoughts are shared, or are transmitted from one person to another, then there is communication. This does not just mean sending messages by speaking and receiving by listening.
   When you are with someone, everything you do and everything about you can send messages between you and become communication. Silence, for instance, can be a most effective means of communication, such as the 'pregnant pause'. Communication can even take place when neither of you is consciously aware of it. For example, you may react by becoming anxious yourself if someone is fidgeting and wringing their hands without really being aware why you are reacting.

Activity

Think about ways in which you communicate feelings or ideas to others. Try to make a list of about five. To start you off, one example is *gesture*. You point to show someone something, for instance, or shrug to show that you do not understand, or wave a hand to emphasize a point you are making.

MEANS OF COMMUNICATION
1 Gesture
2
3
4
5

Everything you do when with another person is part of the communication process. Even before you open your mouth, your dress, appearance and way of walking or standing are sending messages to the other person. So

there are many things which might have been included on your list and our comments only cover some of the ways of communicating.

Speech
Speech is giving instructions and directions, asking questions, making comments, suggestions, giving factual information, or general chat, gossip and jokes.

Style of delivery
Style of delivery is the volume, pitch and stress in your voice. Voice quality can convey a great deal of important information, such as sarcasm or anger, what you are like as a person, how confident or how friendly you are, etc.

Touch or bodily contact
A hug, a caress, or a slap can communicate feelings, including sexual, friendly or aggressive ones. Physical contact is the earliest form of communication used by infants and young children, but in later years it is governed by social restrictions about who can be touched, how and when. Think about the people you don't touch and why.

Body posture and distance
Body posture and distance transmit messages too. Leaning forward or standing close are quite different from the disinterest shown by leaning back in a chair or staying safely behind a barrier, such as a desk.

Gaze or eye contact
Looks convey feelings, particularly of interest or boredom. They also give

away attitudes to people, such as the direct prolonged stare indicating
dominance and the downcast eyes of submission.

Faces

Faces, of course, have a tremendous range of expression for conveying
messages, responses, attitudes and emotions, as you will find in the
following activity.

Activity

This is an exercise designed to help you to observe others and be more aware
of your own social signals. It is based on Trower *et al.* (1978). You need a
partner for this exercise. You could ask someone in your family, a friend or
a colleague to work on this with you.

Take turns to be a partner A or partner B.

Partner A

1 Select two or three face cues from Table 1 (page 24) for one emotion and
   display that emotion.
2 Select one face cue and display it.
3 Select one cue from each of two different emotions and display this as a
   'blend'.

Partner B

1 Guess the emotion expressed and the face cues being used.
2 Guess the emotion and the cue used.
3 Guess the emotions and cues used.

The story of 'Jennifer' that follows shows how surprisingly powerful a
light-hearted game of this kind can be.

Jennifer – making faces

(This story was told to us by a psychologist who saw Jennifer and her
family over a period of time.)

'Jennifer was 13 when I met her, a late child born to parents who were
now nearing retirement. She lived at home attending a special school
for children with moderate mental handicap. She was solemn and
quiet, but often given to angry outbursts which distressed and
bewildered her parents. Other than that, she showed little emotion.

(continued)

At one point a game was introduced. Using mirrors, simple line drawings and our own faces, we played at guessing expressions. Happiness, sadness, fear and anger seemed to be ideas Jennifer had not thought about before. The game itself made her laugh and she soon mastered it. It all seemed a bit trivial at the time, but it had interesting consequences.

Her mother began to watch Jennifer more carefully and to notice cues she hadn't seen before. "It seems strange," she told me, "but I never really thought about Jennifer being worried or jealous or anything like that before." Jennifer became more of a person to her with real feelings and emotions and, of course, that in turn helped Jennifer.

It did not solve all the family's problems at a stroke, of course, but it did seem an important step forward.'

We hope you too enjoyed the experience and learned something of the complexity of human communication. Over the next few days you could try to become a 'person watcher'.

Watch how people move their hands and how they stand; notice eye contact and watch facial expressions; listen to how people talk. Think about what the behaviours convey to you about the other person, and his or her attitudes, feelings and ideas. Also think about what you are doing and all the messages you are sending by your tone of voice, facial expressions, hands and eyes. Bear that in mind as you read this extract by Paul Williams who attempted to present a picture of the world as he thought a person with a mental handicap might see it:

'When one of us meets one of you, especially if it is for the first time, we are quite likely to lack many of the skills for successful communication. We may not be able to think of anything appropriate to say, nor to put it into the right words, or to control our facial expression. But you also will show a great lack of skill. You will be embarrassed, you won't be able to think of anything appropriate to say, you will tend to talk in an inappropriate tone of voice, you will tend to have a wide grin on your face and ask questions without really being interested in the answer. The handicap is thus a mutual one. Both of us have difficulty in communicating with and forming relationships with the other.'

(Williams, 1978)

You will probably agree that he provides a clear description of the two-way process and a useful reminder that it is not just those with a mental handicap who can have difficulty with communication.

INTRODUCING SHARED ACTION PLANNING

Two key questions have emerged:

- How *can* positive two-way relationships be encouraged to offer opportunities for growth and well-being?
- How *can* communication be improved?

This workbook offers some specific ideas and suggestions that you can pick up and try out as you wish. The development of these ideas is framed within the process of Shared Action Planning, designed to offer you a support structure for change.

This structure is flexible and can be used as much or as little as you need; but it is there to help you. It is there also to help ensure that any process of change is a two-way thing. You may want to continue to use this planning process or perhaps try it with other people, particularly if you are in a work setting. You may also want to pass the ideas on to other people. To make this easier, we have developed an Appendix comprised of forms and guidelines explaining how Shared Action Planning can work.

Various people have tried this process out for us too, and one family in particular, the Hawkes, has given us detailed feedback. As you work through the rest of this workbook and try out the planning process for yourself, you will be able to see how the Hawkes reacted, what ideas they developed, and compare notes with them.

Activity

Now read through the 'Forms and Guidelines' in the Appendix. You do not have to take in every detail at the first reading, but you should expect to spend perhaps up to half an hour reading through the guidelines and looking at the information asked for on the five forms. When you have finished, come back to this page to find out how the Hawkes family got on.

*Michael Knight and the Hawkes family: starting
out on their shared Action Plan*

A Shared Action Plan for
Michael Knight and the Hawkes family

This illustrates Michael and the Hawkes's rather stumbling start to something they have found to be hard work but, in their view, very much worth the effort.

Michael is 17 now and has lived with the Hawkes family for three years as their foster son. Peter and Beth Hawkes plan to adopt him next year. They have three children of their own: Tony who is 16, and Mary and Liz who are 9 and 10. They live in a semi-detached house in a small town in the north of England. Michael has only recently left school and is just starting at an Adult Training Centre (ATC) where the emphasis is being put on 'general work skills'. Michael is an active young man and under 'Present Leisure

Activities' they wrote the following: 'Youth Club; cycles; watches TV; plays tape-recorder; plays darts and snooker; plays computer games; takes dogs for walks; visits friends'.

That was the easiest part. They felt much more anxious as they moved on to talking about aims and goals, about 'stirring up waters they might not want to stir'. Conflicts did arise, but as you will see later, they were able to think things through as a result, and to move forward together.

Peter and Beth became the plan co-ordinators identified on Form A (see Appendix), and gradually other key people – a teacher Michael wanted to involve, and later an instructor from the ATC – were brought in too. The forms themselves made Beth groan at first sight, but they persevered. What was it that made them continue? They answered this by talking about their other son, Tony, who is about the same age as Michael. They have similar conflicts with Tony, in fact 'worse at the moment'. But Beth and Peter believe that they will resolve themselves.

'He has all the opportunities. It's just a matter of deciding.' But it's different with Michael. 'We all need to be more *deliberate*. We could see why we would like to have some goals – but it is a matter of getting to *shared* goals, that is the problem.'

Michael himself enjoyed the process especially the time spent talking together – and he enjoyed choosing his own pen-name for this account, after his current television hero, Michael Knight. After Michael agreed to the idea, Peter, Beth and he formed, in effect, a partnership. We shall be asking you too to form a partnership: to invite someone you know with a mental handicap to take part in Shared Action Planning with you, to become *your partner* in trying out this process. If their mental handicap is severe and they are unable to discuss this with you, perhaps somebody else can act as their advocate and protect their interests at all times. Are there any good reasons, they would have to consider, why this person should *not* want to take part? Or does it seem as if it would be to their benefit?

If, for whatever reason, it is not possible to find a partner to co-operate, you will have to make do with your imagination. Perhaps another time you will have a chance to put what you have learned into practice. It is really only by trying out the process together with a partner that you will discover whether it succeeds in what it sets out to do: to provide a way of improving communication; encouraging a positive two-way relationship; and creating new and better opportunities for growth and well-being.

Before asking you to embark on this journey of exploration, because that is really what it is, you might like to know a bit more about what lies behind the Shared Action Plan idea. Various questions have arisen as it has been developed. Some of them might be questions in your mind too.

What's behind the Shared Action Plan idea?

A focus on relationships:

- because the importance of relationships has been too long overlooked for people with mental handicap.
- because relationships are central to any process of growth and development.

A focus on communication:

- because difficulties in communication often lie behind the breakdown in the understanding of what a person with a mental handicap needs
- because communication and understanding can grow and develop between people in circumstances which support and encourage it

Why does it have to be so structured?

Can't people just learn to relax, be friends and enjoy life naturally?

- Sometimes they can – sometimes two-way relationships and a shared approach to life happen spontaneously.
- For many people with mental handicap, however, and for those of you involved closely with them, it is not that easy. All kinds of problems get in the way. The structure of this approach is designed to support your attempts to do just that – to relax, be friends and enjoy life naturally.

Why do there have to be forms to fill in?

- Writing things down helps in all kinds of ways. It helps to organize thoughts and ideas. It helps other people to know what is happening. It helps people to remember and to plan. The forms offer a structure that leads people through a process of shared planning.
- Normally it is the professionals who fill in forms and keep records and files. This tends to mean that they are the ones in control of information and planning. These, in contrast, are *your* forms which may help *you* to feel more in control of decision-making. They may also help you to communicate better with professionals.

Why not just use Individual Programme Planning?

- Shared Action Planning builds on what was good about Individual Programming Planning and it should, therefore, be quite simple to make the transition from using Individual Programme Plans to using Shared Action Plans.
- It does involve a significant shift in approach, however. One person who had been using Individual Programme Planning noticed this: 'It

Normally the professional is in control of information and planning.

made me think differently and I found I was coming up with different goals. I would like to see whether we could use it in the hospital where I work.'

- In Shared Action Planning the perspective of the individual is *built in* to the process.
- Also built in is the need to become aware of, and resolve, conflicting aims or different priorities.
- The process starts with aims so that questions of assessment can be as helpful and relevant as possible.
- It strengthens the contribution to the overall planning process of the individual and those most closely involved.
- It focuses outwards from the individual in looking for change and not just in towards the individual.
- It looks at 'what needs to happen' to achieve shared goals rather than painting a picture of an individual with a list of needs which other people have to meet.

How does it fit in with other developments that are taking place?

- Self-advocacy – Shared Action Planning involves creating a partnership which supports and encourages an individual towards increasing self-advocacy.
- Citizen advocacy – for people not yet able to begin to speak up for themselves, the planning process explicitly recognizes the need for someone to speak on their behalf.
- Normalization – this movement has put an increasing emphasis on creating opportunities for normal lifestyles and relationships, by means which are valued by society and not demeaning to the individual. The changes in attitude and practice which have resulted are a major influence behind the shift to Shared Action Planning.

Isn't it too difficult for 'ordinary' parents, 'ordinary' care workers, or 'ordinary' volunteers?

- You will have to judge that for yourselves. Some of you may find forms off-putting and choose only to become part-way involved in the process. It is intended to be flexible and allow for that. Others, like one of the parents using this approach who had done no studying since leaving school at 15, will take to it with ease and fill the forms full of new ideas and insights.
- The process itself is built on everyday interactions and skills which all of you possess already. Only here, as Beth said, 'we all need to be more deliberate'.

Where does the idea come from?

It comes from a multitude of sources, of course. For those of you who are interested in reading further about some of the ideas behind it, we can mention a few written sources that influenced us. (Complete references are given at the end of the workbook.)

- On relationships: Carl Rogers's book (1978) *On Personal Power*; Perlman's account (1979) *Relationships: the Heart of Helping People*; and Argyle and Henderson's (1985) *The Anatomy of Relationships*
- On Individual Programme Plans: The *Draft Procedural Guide* from Blunden at the Mental Handicap in Wales Applied Research Unit (1980), and an American publication called *Way to Go*
- On advocacy and self-advocacy: the book by Williams and Schoultz (1982) called *We Can Speak for Ourselves*; Sang and O'Brien's book on *Advocacy* (1984); some of the ideas from the book by Cooper and Hersov on *Self-Advocacy* (1986)
- On normalization: A substantial book edited by Flynn and Nitsch

(1980); or nearer home by Tyne and O'Brien (1982) *The Principle of Normalisation* from the Campaign for Mentally Handicapped People

- Finally, on how people learn, we mention two texts out of a huge literature available, because these two both provide careful and readable summaries from different perspectives: first, by Blunden and Revill (1980), a unit in another Open University course, 'A Behavioural Approach'; second, a delightful book by Guy Claxton (1984) called *Live and Learn*.

Activity

Before you leave this chapter of the workbook, can you make your first approach to someone you would like to be your partner? Jot down some notes first about how you will try to explain what it is about. Do this even if the person you have in mind has no language. You can check back through this chapter to find some of the reasons we have offered. Don't forget that one of the main reasons is to help *you* study this approach.

WILL YOU BE MY PARTNER IN THIS, BECAUSE...

-

-

-

-

When you have an opportunity, raise the question with the person you have chosen, or with somebody who can try to take on the role of advocate and speak on his or her behalf. As part of your discussion, read through Form A together and the guidance notes in paragraph 4.1 of the 'Forms and Guidelines' (see Appendix for both).

Jot down some rough notes as you start thinking about it:

- Who would be the *key people* the two of you would want to share the plan with?

● Who could be the two *plan co-ordinators*?

● Do you want or need a *plan consultant* at this stage who can offer advice?

● Who else might help? (*Other contributors*)

● Who would you want to keep in touch? (*Circulation list* for papers)

● What are your partner's present living arrangements?

● Present educational or work arrangements?

● Present work activities?

When you both feel ready, fill in Form A, and your partnership in Shared Action Planning has begun.

In Chapter 2 we shall be beginning to think about what you and your partner would most like to see happening next.

Table 1	Facial cues		
	Brows	*Eyes*	*Mouth*
Surprise	brows raised	eyes wide open	mouth open, relaxed
Fear	brows drawn together and raised	eyes wide open	mouth corners drawn back
Anger	brows lowered	eyes wide open	lips pressed together
Sadness	brows lowered at corners	eyes lowered	mouth corners up
Happiness	neutral	'crows feet' creases	mouth corners up

CHAPTER 2
AIMS AND GOALS:
A SENSE OF DIRECTION

Aims and goals are important to people because they are to do with hope. They suggest that new possibilities exist and that choices can be made. Although there are overlaps, *aims* usually refer to general long-term intentions, and *goals* to more specific short-term intentions. It is helpful to link the two: aims setting a general sense of direction for the next few years, such as a wish to create more leisure opportunities for you and your family; goals providing some specific first steps to be achieved in the direction of the general aim, in this case perhaps to decide on two possible family activities and try each of them once over the next month. We shall come back to goals later in this section. First the focus is on *aims*.

The question asked on Appendix Form B to help you to think about your aims is 'What would people most like to see happening over the next few years?' and there is space on the form for each person involved to have an answer recorded. This is a deceptively simple question. To answer it can take a lot of thought and discussion.

Usually we talk about aims for the person with mental handicap, sometimes trying to discover what his or her own aims and wishes are, but often imposing our own ideas on them. Here we are deliberately starting with *you*, asking you to reflect on your own aims. There are two reasons for this. First, an awareness of what your personal aims are can help everyone, including you, to know where they stand in relation to other people's aims. Your aims may conflict, for example, with the aims of the person with mental handicap, or with somebody else involved, and it is important to recognize and discuss such problems. Second, it can help in understanding how another person works out his or her aims and what the process feels like. You realize then what a complex task it is.

Staff who have been involved in trying to reach agreed aims and goals with individuals and families told us:

> 'To start with we were so naïve. We just thought we could bounce in and ask people what they wanted. But, of course, they didn't know what was important to them or what might help. They didn't know what they were meant to say – "to be a film star" or what? It needed about six months really just getting to know each other.'

The people involved here were starting from scratch, whereas most of you will already be in the position of being involved within your own family or with other individuals and their families. Nevertheless, it is still a complex task trying to answer the question 'What would you like to see happening?' in satisfactory terms for yourself and also with, or on behalf of, your partner. It is a task that may raise as many questions as it answers. In this chapter we shall be working through some of these questions, suggesting that you make notes as you go along. This will help you build ideas and skills, so that at the end you can make a thought-out attempt at completing Appendix Form B on behalf of yourself and your partner.

DEVELOPING AWARENESS

First we are going to consider some basic questions about aims. It is a good idea to make your own notes about yourself in the notebook, ringbinder or file which you are keeping. These questions won't be full-fledged activities, more a technique to encourage you to 'think aloud' on paper as you go along.

Aims and real life

We have suggested that aims are important to people, but some of you may wonder how big a part they really play in your day-to-day life.

Are you conscious of having aims in your day-to-day life?

ARE THERE SOME OBVIOUS ONES?

Perhaps you will have conscious aims and will have no difficulty in saying what you want to happen. They may be major things such as getting married or a home of your own; or more specific such as passing some exams, learning to drive a car; or more general such as friendships, health, enjoyment. Or perhaps you don't have explicit aims.

You may feel that things will just happen as they happen, or that on the whole you have got what you want out of life. You are still likely to have working assumptions, that is, certain basic expectations about life which will influence the way you behave. Statements such as 'I just assumed I'd get married and have children', 'I never thought I'd be out of a job and on the scrap heap at fifty-four', 'You don't appreciate good health until you've lost it' suggest that people do have expectations about how their lives will be, even if these are not thought-out aims.

Hopes and fears

Moving from basic expectations to defining aims involves an increasing awareness of choices and possibilities that exist. Sometimes that happens in a positive way, as when we are inspired by seeing what somebody else has managed to achieve, and we decide to try to copy them. Sometimes it may be more negative in the sense that we aim to escape from some unpleasant possibility.

DO SOME OF YOUR AIMS OR EXPECTATIONS ARISE OUT OF HOPES AND FEARS?

WHAT IS THE BEST AND WHAT IS THE WORST THAT COULD HAPPEN?

Sometimes when people become very wrapped up in trying to avoid unpleasantness they lose sight of what they would like in its place. Trying to find a positive aim can often be helpful in trying to break a downward spiral of this kind.

In the following story of Jill, you can see how the introduction of a microcomputer into her classroom provided her with a positive aim with remarkable effects.

Jill

'Jill is 17, has Down's Syndrome and attends a school in Northern Ireland for pupils with severe learning difficulties.

When she was twelve she became very cut-off. No one knows why, but she talked less and less with her teachers and the others in her class. She seemed to adopt a "speak only when you're spoken to" attitude. Also, she did not want to have a go at anything new and her story-writing became very repetitive.

It happened that a BBC computer was brought into the classroom just over a year ago and it has played a significant part in helping Jill get on with others in her class. The class worked together first on a program called FACEMAKER which allowed them to put together pictures of faces by choosing from a range of features. Jill gradually began to take an interest and a greater part in class discussions. She started using new words she was learning from the program when talking to others. Another program she got interested in was the TREE OF KNOWLEDGE. She worked with growing confidence and slowly involved others in her work, asking them questions and drawing them into discussions. Jill began to take a pride in her work and to enjoy demonstrating programs on the computer to her friends.

It seems to her teachers that through using the computer Jill has:

- started her own projects and worked systematically on them
- talked more with other pupils in her class and her teachers
- developed her abilities in using and understanding language
- developed her reading and writing abilities
- enjoyed and taken pride in all that she has done'

(From an account by Alan Nixon, courtesy of the Council for Educational Technology, 3 Devonshire Street, London W1N 2BA)

Striving and contentment

How much importance do you attach to future expectations and how much do you concentrate on enjoying the here and now?

FUTURE EXPECTATIONS

ENJOYMENT OF THE PRESENT

A balance is obviously needed. The support worker, for example, who is determined a resident will learn to be independent in personal care, may forget the pleasures to be had from the process of living and learning itself. On the other hand, we are seldom completely unaware of longer-term possibilities. Parents of children with a mental handicap, for example, who 'take one day at a time' are still very conscious of the fears for the future which they are blotting out.

Concentrating on what you like now, what is good about your present life, can not only help to make you more aware of the positive aspects of your life; it can also be a sound starting point for thinking ahead – to what you would like to see happening. But we still have to be careful about the balance. Sometimes a complete change is needed rather than some careful step-by-step building from a bad starting point.

WHAT KINDS OF AIM?

People may have different kinds of aim. They can answer questions about aims in very different ways. It will also depend on the way the questions are phrased.

Where on earth to start is one common problem in trying to arrive at some sensible aims. What is a 'reasonable' aim? Let us have a look at what might have been the aims of some of the people who feature in the P555 course, 'Mental Handicap: Patterns for Living'.

When Shirley was 36 years old, she was living in a 25-bedded purpose-built hostel and had been there since her mother died. Her Social Services file indicated that she was an 'obvious choice' for the hostel's training unit. Shirley, however, had had a rough passage and what she seemed to want at that stage was to settle into her niche in the hostel and feel reasonably content.

Mrs Turnbull was under a lot of pressure caring for her severely handicapped daughter Tracey. 'She needs a lot of attention. She is hard work. It's not just the physical hard work that wears me out though. Tracey cries a lot, sometimes she screams and often she has disturbed nights. The worst thing of all is that she doesn't appear to recognize me or know who I am...' What she wanted was a situation where she could still love and care for Tracey, but where some of the chores were shared by other people.

Melvyn Jarvis is 22 years old and has lived in a hospital for people with a mental handicap since he was three. Melvyn, who is severely handicapped with virtually no hearing or sight, was at one stage very 'touch defensive'. That is, he resisted any physical contact with anybody or anything. It seemed, as far as we can judge, that he wanted to feel safe and unthreatened.

Philip and Cynthia Taylor now live in a bungalow with a small garden. They have lived there since their wedding six years ago. Before that, when they lived in a hospital for people with a mental handicap, they were consistent in their wish to marry and live in the community.

How do you react to each of these apparent aims? Are they 'reasonable' aims for them to have?

SHIRLEY GRANT

MRS TURNBULL

MELVYN JARVIS

THE TAYLORS

Shirley Grant
What were some of the reactions to these aims? First about Shirley:

She has to achieve that goal of feeling secure and happy first.

I feel she has some idea of what she would like.

The feeling was that her wishes should be respected in the first instance.

On the other hand, some people said it did not seem right because they felt it was shutting out possibilities that might expand her life.

Would accepting her wish seem like accepting her limited view of herself? Should she be helped to reach out for something more? There might be other conflicts too, like wanting to free a hostel place to move someone else out of hospital.

Mrs Turnbull

Most people asked felt happy with Mrs Turnbull's aims:

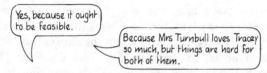

Yet it was not feasible – not for a long time. If the Turnbulls wanted Tracey at home they just had to manage. If not – well the answer was a special boarding school more than a hundred miles away. Until the hostel was built there was no other option. What would you have made of Mrs Turnbull's aims if the help she was seeking didn't exist?

One person felt that the demands on Mrs Turnbull would be too great in the long run and the aim should be independence through gradual separation.

Melvyn Jarvis

We all, to an extent, wish to avoid frightening experiences. The problem with Melvyn's wish not to be touched is that he keeps out everything else as well. He closes off all opportunities to relate to people, or to learn anything new. So you probably felt this wouldn't do as an aim. It runs contrary to too many other aims. Many people, when asked, felt this too.

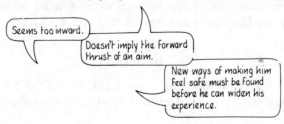

In fact, what happened was that the aim of making contact with Melvyn and widening his experience was seen as more appropriate, but this only became possible because his wishes and fears *were* recognized. The contact had to be made without frightening him. This was done by, for instance, giving him a warning from the gentle puff of air from the fan to let him know that someone was there.

The Taylors
When asked, most people had no hesitations about the Taylors' aims.

> It is their wish, their right and it seems realistic.

> Their aims are natural, human and achievable.

However, a few years ago, you may have said that their aims were unrealistic. It's easy to say 'yes' now, knowing that they did make it. At the time the hospital staff were in no doubt that the answer was 'no'. Philip was even moved to a hostel to separate him from Cynthia. They couldn't imagine that such an idea could succeed. Their own aims for the Taylors were much less amibitious.

The aims which we have been discussing were all quite different from each other, although they could all be seen as answers to the question 'What would you like to see happening...?' Given that people's aims can range so widely, it would seem helpful if there were some sort of framework you could turn to. That is what Appendix Form B provides.

Overall aims and direction: Form B

Three simple but comprehensive areas are suggested in Form B:

* living arrangements
* educational and work opportunities
* leisure arrangements

More detailed questions to run through in your mind as you consider possible aims are laid out in sections 5.1–5.3 of the Appendix.

Activity

Think about your own aims for a bit. Look at sections 5.1–5.3 of the 'Forms and Guidelines' in the Appendix which sets out a range of questions under the headings of Living Arrangements, Education and Work Opportunities, and Leisure Arrangements. If possible find somebody you can trust to talk to, and spend some time discussing what you feel *you* might like to see happening over the next few years in any of these areas. Jot down any ideas you come up with and some notes about why they seem important to you.

YOUR IDEAS AND WHY THEY SEEM IMPORTANT

In constructing this framework (living arrangements, educational and work opportunities and leisure arrangements) we were aware that the three areas were unlikely to cover every eventuality – life isn't that easy to pigeon-hole. What we have tried to do is to help set a direction for your thinking in tune with the principles of normalization. The checklists are to help you skim through a whole series of issues that might be important and pick out the ones that are. But they are also intended to direct your thoughts towards patterns of living in a way which includes ideas about circumstances, and opportunities, as well as skills, abilities and behaviour patterns – other people's as well as your own. This is a move away from the tendency which exists in some approaches to concentrate mainly on the skills, abilities and achievements of the person concerned. To have the focus so much on people's abilities often seems demeaning to the individual concerned.

We hope that, in contrast, you will find this approach reasonably comfortable and helpful to use, even though it involves you in thinking about some quite personal issues.

CULTIVATING AIMS

We have talked about how widely aims can vary. It is also true that, within a given society, there can be surprising similarities in people's aims. You inevitably build your aims as you go along, watching others, absorbing the values of your culture and matching those observations with your own experiences of pleasure and satisfaction.

You learn as you go along, testing out ideas and finding out what seems to work for you, what seems possible, and what desirable. And you do it with others who are part of your life and experiences. You learn through others what the possibilities are and what you may reasonably expect for yourself. There are no right answers and you may not always accept what is reflected back to you, but you listen and judge it.

What happens in this process when the person has a mental handicap?
People with mental handicap are no different in this. They, too, will learn from others how to consider and develop their own possibilities. Unfortunately, the label itself may lead to other people having low expectations of them. The possibilities painted may be restricted and impoverished, and they are taught slowly but surely to set their own aims low.

In the case of people with a mental handicap the boundaries of our imagination have been very restricted. A very limited range of possibilities has been considered by planners and providers of services, and as a result goals have been set within those patterns of expectation. Until relatively recently when new and more effective ways of helping people to learn were developed, care remained the only goal. With the new ideas about learning came new possibilities. People, who in the past had been thought quite unable to learn, showed they could learn. With appropriate education, started early enough, it seemed that many people might now be capable of achieving far more. Goals were then set firmly in the realms of learning and development.

The philosophy of normalization, with its emphasis on making normal life experiences accessible to mentally handicapped people, has shifted the boundaries of imagination still further, with the result that new possibilities have emerged. For many people like the Taylors, these are not such new ideas. They had no difficulty in imagining they could live like other people, given a bit of necessary help. For many others the shift is still a difficult one to make and some aims still seem impossible to achieve.

Activity

An aim has to be achievable; you have to believe it's possible. Are there aims or goals that you now feel are possible for your partner that you would not have considered a few years ago? Are there some that still seem impossible?

NEW POSSIBILITIES   STILL IMPOSSIBLE

You may have included possibilities like jobs, control of money, even marriage or a home of his or her own. What about having children? Did you hesitate there? Or perhaps your partner is more severely handicapped and the possibilities you thought of were more restricted than these.

Perhaps some aims seemed too unrealistic to include. The principles of normalization suggest that if experiences are valued by most people in our society, then they are probably a good guide for us in imagining possibilities for people with mental handicap. But is it always fair to aim so high when some possibilities may seem beyond people's reach?

Perhaps there are two kinds of answer to this question – answers which people are discovering together:

- First, more things are possible than were ever dreamed of a few years ago. Limits on expectations have been clearly wrong. Perhaps they are still wrong. Many people can do far more, achieve more, enjoy more and aim higher than had ever been imagined. This kind of answer will lead to aims which focus on the possibilities of increased skills and greater independence.

- The second kind of answer has to do with valuing people equally for what they are and the need to reconsider some of society's values. People can find fulfilment in different patterns of living. Looking for individual aims can help us to piece together what those patterns are for an individual.This way of thinking may lead to aims which involve the pleasure and satisfaction gained from friendships and activities. Skills and independence may play a part in this for some people, but they may not be the first priority.

Activity

Look back over the notes about your aims you jotted down in the activity on page 33. Did your ideas for yourself reflect both these approaches: a striving towards greater skills and competence on the one hand, and a wish for pleasure and contentment through enjoyable relationships and activities on the other?

Did your aims show:
(a) more emphasis on increasing your skills in some way?
(b) more emphasis on increasing your level of contentment and enjoyment?
(c) a balance between the two?

On the whole the more you emphasize skills the more you are asking of *yourself*, and the more you emphasize enjoyment the more you may be asking of *other people*. This activity is here simply to draw your attention to these differences in approach in relation to your own aims, before you move on now to thinking about the aims of the person with mental handicap.

It is your turn now to offer support to someone else while he or she tries to clarify his or her aims just as you have done. How you approach this will depend a lot on your relationship with the other person, his or her age and ability to use spoken language and to think ahead. If you were using this approach in reality, and not just as an exercise to try it out, you might well have the help of another key person and you would certainly have a longer time-scale.

Activity

What might you try with your partner in order to stretch ideas and discuss possibilities?

THINGS TO TRY

Perhaps your partner needs to learn more about what possibilities there might be:

- Does your partner need more information? Can he or she ask? Can you tell him or her things?
- Does your partner need to see more examples of what might happen? Can he or she look at pictures with you? Can he or she see how other people do things?
- Does your partner need to try things out – find out what it feels like to swim, go on a bus, have a picnic, be alone, have a friend?

Remember Melvyn. At one time he had no experience or awareness of the possibility of being approached or touched without fear, or learning that people can become familiar and experiences can be fun. The process of opening up a world of possibilities for Melvyn included being part of a small group of residents assigned to two members of staff, Jean and Doreen. They spent time with him and took a personal interest in him, his appearance and activities. He has begun to enjoy experiences now, particularly his regular outings to the swimming pool.

Remember Shirley. She seemed to have lost confidence in herself. The process of emerging as a decisive person able to speak up for herself included becoming a member of a self-advocacy group. Two attempts had been made to move her from the hostel: first, into a unit with four other residents and, then, into a house shared with a volunteer. Both attempts failed. The self-advocacy group concentrates on consciousness-raising and self-assertion, and Shirley now asserts that she is ready to leave the hostel. She wants to live in a flat on her own.

Could you have helped to draw out Melvyn or Shirley?

You will, of course, be influencing your partner's ideas. That is how things happen. It is what happens to all of us. It is a problem which has to be recognized, but on balance it seems better to try to expand and stretch someone's horizons, than to sit tight and do nothing for fear of influencing his or her decisions.

But remember, too, that you may have to stretch your own horizons. Do *you* believe Shirley can manage alone? Would *you* have accepted the Taylors' wish to marry?

Talking about aims may not be possible, or at least it may not be enough. You will have to develop empathy: to notice the feelings and reactions of the other person; and look for clues about what feels good or right to him or her.

Communication, as we saw earlier, is not just to do with what people say. A lot of communication happens through the way people behave, their tone of voice, facial expression, body posture, attention and direction of gaze.

Think about yourself for a minute, and the situations that make you feel good. How do you show it? Is it easy for others to see how you are feeling? And what about your partner. Even with someone you know intimately, you may still find there are moods and feelings you only notice when you look more closely.

These clues can help you and your partner to discover what he or she would most like to happen.

Activity

What are the clues that might suggest somebody is feeling good?

JOT DOWN YOUR IDEAS – THINKING OF
YOURSELF AND YOUR PARTNER IN PARTICULAR

Here is our list of 'feeling good' indicators:

- saying so with words or other sounds
- smiling
- paying attention
- looking alert and interested
- laughing out loud
- taking part enthusiastically
- looking confident – head up
- making good eye contact
- absence of frowning/worried or depressed expression
- body relaxed but alert
- looking comfortable
- staying in the situation
- making you feel good

Activity

What would your partner like to see happening over the next few years?
Piece together the evidence of what your partner is able to tell you through words, or any of the other clues listed above. Again, jot down your rough ideas first. Put yourself in your partner's shoes and try not to ignore any aims you disagree with at this stage. You need as clear a picture as possible of what seems important from your partner's point of view.

Use the question guidelines in sections 5.1–5.3 of the 'Forms and Guidelines' appendix again to help you both to consider a range of possible areas:

LIVING ARRANGEMENTS

WORK OR EDUCATIONAL OPPORTUNITIES

LEISURE ACTIVITIES

This kind of activity really needs more time than you can give to it as you work through this workbook. It's really a part of a continuing process of discovering possibilities.

Looking at what you have jotted down, though, can you see whether you have a balance there between developing skills and finding enjoyment? Of course, they often come together, but you might like to think again if your focus is heavily on skills development. Ask yourself why, and how *you* would have felt.

Activity

Completing Form B

Now you are almost ready to make some entries on Form B. Just to remind you, it asks first, 'What would people most like to see happening over the next few years?' and provides spaces for key people's answers to be recorded against living arrangements, educational and work opportunities, and leisure activities.

So far you have:

- made notes on what *you* would like to see happening (on p. 33)
- made notes on what *your partner* would like to see happening (on p. 39)

First write *your partner's* aims on to the form. That should be reasonably straightforward.

With your *own* aims, you may want to think a bit more before writing them on the form. The Shared Action Plan is really your partner's plan, so now you need to think about your aims, or what you would like to see happening, as they relate to your partner. Have a look through your notes again and consider whether the ideas you jotted down do relate in this way or not. Underline the points that *do* seem relevant. Anything that will affect your relationship, your attitude, the time you can spend together, your

Form B: OVERALL AIMS AND DIRECTION

MICHAEL_____ 's SHARED ACTION PLAN   Date form completed ___3rd April 1986___
(NAME)

What would people most like to see happening over the next few years?

(This form should be drawn up by the plan co-ordinators with the <u>key people</u> (which may include themselves) over a period of time. See guidance notes.)

Names of key people:	Michael	Peter	Beth
1 <u>In terms of living arrangements?</u>	To live in a house by myself - nearby so I can pop in.	I'd like him to live within us for a few years and when he's ready and sensible about looking after himself to choose where he lives?	I'd like him to live with us and learn to understand all about looking after a home, with a view to him being an independent on his own.
2 <u>In terms of educational and work arrangements?</u>	I'd like to work in a shop or work with horses. I think I'd be better with horses. I know all about horses.	I'd like him to settle in to the ATC for a year or two than about working for a job - maybe with horses, but there are other things he might like.	I'd like him to be as successful at the ATC, what ways feel he needs to move on then I'd like him to do a course on people work to help him get a job.
3 <u>In terms of leisure activities?</u>	Ride a moped. Join a football club and a snooker club.	I'd like him to do the same things as me and join a football and snooker club and the moped. Go to football on his own.	I'd like him to have things to do so he's not bored - to be able to go out for a game of badminton or phone a friend and arrange to meet.
POSSIBLE STARTING POINTS: (GOALS) (NOTE: Are there areas of agreement where you could identify some goals to aim at over the next six months or so? Try to find at least one, but no more than three.)	1. Try out local sports facilities 2. Keep clean and tidy, aware of appearance without reminders. 3. Renew contact with Scouts stabler 4. Buy and learn to ride a moped		Explain briefly why you have focused on each goal and how it relates to overall (longer-term) aims. 1. Keen sportsman, but few opportunities since leaving school. Increase social circle. 2. Keen to be attractive to people - wants to feel grown-up, worried about spots. Important for independent living. 3. Keen horseman and it relates with work opportunities/relationships. 4. Increase chances of getting around on his own - more independence and safer.
Rejected goals	1. Manage own money 2. To be honest - not telling lies so much.		Explain reason for rejection, e.g. conflict, difficulty, non-availability of service. 1. Too difficult for now. Too much hassle, not worth it at the moment. Would clash with saving for moped. 2. Michael aggressive, needs time to think how to tackle it.

ability to cope and so on will be relevant, as well as any more direct links.

Also are there any aims you want to add now; things *you* would like to see happening *to or for* your partner specifically? This, of course, would usually be the starting point and may feel more comfortable and familiar to you. But what you now have gained is a greater awareness of your own wishes and how they match or compete with your wishes for the other person.

Now you can enter your aims on to Form B. There is space on the form for a third or fourth key person to have his or her ideas entered, but unless you are working with others at the moment there is no need to complete that as part of this exercise.

The Hawkes family and Michael Knight filled in their form after some considerable debate (more of that later). It is copied in full on page 40.

Do you have any reactions to it? The process itself made *them* think and they discuss that too a little later.

FROM AIMS TO GOALS

At the start of this chapter, we suggested that goals could be seen as more specific statements of intent over a shorter period. You now have an idea of what at least you and your Action Plan partner would like to see happening over the next few years, but can you now find some areas of agreement and arrive at some more immediate goals to aim for over the next few months. First, what about agreement?

Agreement and conflict

Peter and Beth Hawkes told us in a tape-recorded discussion how it took a lot of talking to arrive at agreement with Michael about their aims and goals. They were all agreed that their first four Shared Action Plan meetings were hard work. The arguments and conflicts were so bad at times that they nearly gave up. So what caused the disagreements and how did they resolve matters?

Do you write down whatever the person with a mental handicap says? What if you believe that it is not what the person really wants or thinks? Michael said he wanted to live on his own. Both Peter and Beth felt he was not saying what he really wanted. He was testing them out. But then they did not agree about what they should do. Peter said that to write it down would spoil the Shared Action Plan. How could they plan on the basis of what he doesn't want? Beth, on the other hand, said that they must put

down what Michael says. How could it be his plan if they didn't? So there
was conflict all round.

In the end, they recorded what Michael said. Peter felt better when he and
Beth recorded their views next to Michael's, that is that they would like him
to live with them for a few years. And Michael shifted his views a little when
he knew what *they* had written. That seemed to make sense to him. They
also came up later with the idea of making rough notes. This helped them all
say what they wanted to say, knowing that they could change their minds
and work on it before it went on the form.

Another problem was: 'You know it's wrong but you want to think so
much for him – because he's not sensible enough to think for himself, I
suppose.' Peter's understandable attitude again brought conflicts between
himself and Beth and Michael. Beth and Peter also found it difficult not to
'turn it into a lecture, even though you're kicking yourself after'. It is the
'Well, that shows you why. . .' trap. Michael had said he wanted a moped
and that triggered off a 'Well, that shows you why . . . you need to look
after your money and not smoke so much', and so on. 'Michael saw it as
more of an earful than a Shared Action Plan', and he told them so . . . and
there was more conflict.

A number of things improved matters:

- having another person involved to help Michael put his side
- realizing that nothing happens overnight; this is not a snap solution to
  long-running problems
- agreeing *shared* goals with give and take from everyone involved

Resolving conflicts and finding compromises is something you are
continually involved in. Life is like that. People's needs, rights, wishes and
desires continually compete for attention and cut across each other. To call
this a Shared Action Plan is not to pretend that all is sweetness and light and
that everybody will agree on what should happen.

A good starting point is to focus on areas where there is agreement. There
can be a fair measure of agreement about the general direction in which
things should be moving. But what happens when there are conflicting
aims? How can you and your partner then reach agreement about aims?
The important first step is to have opened up communication.

An Open University community education course, 'Parents and
Teenagers', suggests ways of reducing conflict and negotiating with people:

Being genuine
Being open and honest about yourself, your aims and your limitations.

Showing respect
Trying to see another person as that person is now, in his or her own right.

Taking your time
Not being in too much of a hurry. Everyone needs time to talk openly about his or her feelings and ideas. Listening takes time too.

Do some of these sound familiar to you? We might add:

Try to put yourself in their shoes
Think about what your partner is really trying to say. Perhaps Michael Knight was really saying he wanted to see himself as adult and independent in the long run, rather than actually wanting to leave home as soon as possible.

What about the goals themselves? This is going to involve making judgements about which goals are most appropriate. So who makes the judgements and on what basis do they make them?

In Shared Action Planing, provisional goals should be agreed by the small group of people drawing up aims *before* any larger meeting takes place. It is usually in small discussions of two or three key people that compromises can best be reached and judgements made. There will still be a tendency for those most accustomed to thinking and planning ahead to influence and direct the judgements. There may be situations where the person whose plan it is is unable to contribute to this process. Whether that is the case or not, at least, his or her aims are there on paper to be taken into account. More usually some input will be possible, and in many cases a little experience leads to a situation where the individuals see this process of selecting priorities as very much theirs to lead.

Apart from who makes the judgements, there is still the question of the basis for making judgements. What might influence this choice?

Agreement
It may reflect an area of agreement about aims, e.g. that some friendships and support outside the family are desirable.

Achievability
It may seem a goal which is easily achievable, for example, that the next-door neighbour will act as a companion on outings twice a week.

Availability
It may be a goal that fits in with existing services and styles of working, for example, that a place has just been offered in an adult education class and should be taken up.

Importance

It may seem really important to the individual, for example, that she really wants to go out with someone her own age.

Activity

Think about some possible goals to put on your form and make some notes. Start by concentrating on areas of agreement and talking (if that is appropriate) with your Shared Action Plan partner about possible goals. If necessary, talk further about finding compromises for areas of disagreement. Listen hard and try to understand your partner's point of view.

Goals are often described, on Individual Programme Plans (IPP) for example, as statements of what an outcome must be for an individual, such as 'John will learn to travel to the ATC by bus on his own every day'. Chapter 4 will discuss this in more detail, but here we would like to use goals in the broader sense to include any kind of outcome. This is to avoid the danger of ending up with a set of rather patronizing statements about what someone else, in this case your partner, *ought* to do to bring about *self-improvement*. Using Shared Action Plans should help you to avoid that particular trap.

POSSIBLE GOALS:

You could use the following checklist for the possible goals you have noted down.

- Are they based on agreed aims?
- Are the goals agreed with your Shared Action Plan partner?
- Are they clear and specific so that anyone could understand what you mean?
- Do they refer to something that can probably happen within the next six months or less?
- Are different kinds of goals included? They should not all focus on the need for the individual to improve his or her skills, for example.
- Were any goals rejected because they conflicted with other goals? If so, make a note of them and the reason.
- Were any rejected because they seemed too difficult? Again, note them for future reference.
- Were any rejected because the necessary services or help did not seem to be available? If so write it down and let somebody know! Some IPP schemes send a formal notification to the appropriate authority when a required service is not available.

When you are happy with your notes, enter your chosen goals and your rejected goals, together with the reasons, on to Form B.

Congratulations, you have now completed Chapter 2.

CHAPTER 3
ASSESSMENT: COMING TO UNDERSTAND EACH OTHER

WHAT IS ASSESSMENT

Assessment is a process of building up pictures; trying to make sense of yourself, the people around you, and the circumstances you find yourself in. Such pictures help you to make sense of what happens around you, to know what to expect from yourself and from others, and to plan how you should behave.

In general terms, assessment is something we all do with each other as a part of the two-way process of communication. We watch, discuss and negotiate with each other, forming impressions and making judgements. Assessment in this two-way sense is not just a case of you coming to understand another person. It is a sharing of ideas, in which you both gain understanding of yourselves, your circumstances, and each other.

To improve on the assessments that you and your partner make, you must therefore improve your communication and understanding. This is our starting point in this chapter.

IMPROVING COMMUNICATION

Being together

Getting to know each other takes time; time to do things together, and to discuss and share ideas. It can take time, too, to show that you are concerned, and that you are actively interested and listening. This is always important, but especially so when someone has difficulty with communication.

When you think of someone like Tracey with her severe mental handicap, unable to talk or apparently to understand language and with limited movement, how could you begin to discover what her own picture is of herself? How does she see the world? Can we genuinely reach a shared understanding? There is obviously a need to communicate in some way, but, for Tracey, simply talking is not likely to be very easy or productive. Communication will have to be based on shared activities and shared experiences so that each becomes able to read the other's signs.

Activity

Here are some activities which you might share with someone like Tracey. Think of another idea for every one of ours and write it in the second column.

SOME OF OUR SUGGESTIONS	SOME OF YOUR SUGGESTIONS
Going swimming	
Eating ice-cream	
Playing with a dog	
Listening to music	
Going for walks	
Making noises	
Bursting balloons	
Blowing bubbles	
Hiding things	
Playing peep-bo	
Tickling and cuddling	
Making toast	
Splashing in the sink	
Feeding the ducks	

Creating situations you can share is part of a process of getting to know each other. It allows you to see:

● what someone notices and reacts to
● what they seem to like or not like
● what they try to do
● what they manage to do
● what they seem to understand
● how they show their reactions and feelings
● how they react to you in different situations

Look back at our list of activities to share and the items you wrote down. You've probably done all of these things with another person at one time or another. Choose any items on the list where you can easily recall a specific occasion. Just let your mind go over what you found out about the other person, what you think that person might have found out about you, and what you found out about yourself.

Now, the *next* time you are actively involved with somebody in this way, think about what you can learn from it. Be a 'person watcher' and use the list above to help you think about the experience carefully, both while it is going on, and afterwards. But think about yourself too and your own behaviour. What might the other person have found out about you? What kind of picture would he or she have? And what have you found out about yourself? Use the same list of questions for yourself.

Using communication skills

We began exploring the two-way process of communication in Chapter 1. Look back at your list of ways in which we communicate. Have you been a little more aware of what people do when they are together and the messages that are sent? Have you been a 'person watcher'? Your observations will help you in this section where we look at some possibilities for improving communication skills.

Careful *listening* is the key to good communication. A good listener makes you feel you have something worth saying, that you are a person worth taking notice of. Listening is something we learn to do in childhood, but it can continue to improve in adult life.

Activity

Are you a good listener? Good listening skills include: spending time with the other person; taking an interest in what is being said; concentrating on what the person does as well as says; and responding to the person, by providing prompts and words of encouragement. But we all have difficulties listening at some time. Make a short list of times when you know you find it difficult to listen.

TIMES WHEN IT IS DIFFICULT FOR YOU TO LISTEN

Some examples are:

- Lack of time can be a problem. 'This reminds me of when my son was small, and a chatterbox. He used to follow me around from room to room, as I was setting the table, etc., saying: "Just let me tell you this".'
- Your feelings can interfere with listening. 'When I have an urgent problem on my mind.'
- Sometimes reactions to the speaker or what the speaker is saying can make it difficult to listen. 'Boring speaker.'
- Finally, you might have mentioned difficulties in just keeping quiet, suspending judgement and listening to the whole story. 'Perhaps I didn't have as much patience as I thought.'

Activity

This activity is designed to make you more aware of what you do when listening (it is adapted from the Open University course, 'Parents and Teenagers'). Perhaps you can try it out with one of your family or a friend, taking it in turns to be listener and speaker, or it could be fun as a group activity.

The listener has to try to pay attention to the speaker. Encourage the speaker to keep talking and make it clear that you are listening, without using any words. Your face may be particularly important. Do you remember the Activity in Chapter 1? A smile, or raised eyebrows, can mean, 'Go on, I'm listening'. The speaker should talk for three minutes on one of the following topics:

- the best things that happened to me last week
- the things I like and dislike about my job or my life
- my favourite hobby

After about three minutes, change roles and repeat the activity. Then make a list of the things you felt you did as listeners to show that you were paying attention.

THINGS THE LISTENERS SEEMED TO DO:
-
-
-
-
-

Often people feel embarrassed and awkward, or else collapse with laughter, when they first try this. It feels unnatural to practise a skill in this way. But it can increase your awareness of your behaviour. Your list might have included the following:

● Face the speaker.
● Adopt an open posture.
● Lean towards the speaker.
● Maintain eye contact.
● Touch, in some circumstances, can help.
● Have an interested expression.
● React to what is being said.

These ways of showing you are listening can be overdone of course. You should above all be relaxed and calmly paying attention.

This activity can also be tried with the 'listener' pretending not to listen, looking bored and paying no attention to the speaker. You could try this too, if you have time. This time you will be more aware of the effect on you as the speaker. It's hard to keep talking if your 'listener' does not seem interested. If you think about it you will notice that you are more talkative with people who are good, encouraging listeners than you are with others who seem wrapped up in themselves.

You may need to think about this in relation to your partner in the Shared Action Plan. Sometimes a handicap can make it difficult to be a good listener. There may be difficulties in concentrating, or in controlling facial expression or body posture to show attentiveness. There may be different kinds of reactions, especially if there are additional handicaps such as blindness or hearing difficulties. Someone may hear you speaking but be unable to distinguish the words. A blind child will tend to go quiet with head down in order to listen, which can look like a turning away. Parents have to learn to interpret such behaviour and to recognize when their child is trying to pay attention.

Communication skill, here, involves not misinterpreting your partner's listening, not letting yourself be put off just because you don't at first seem to get a response. It also involves thinking about the messages you are giving. If you are not being listened to or understood, perhaps you need to change your approach. You could look back at the section on 'Being Together'. Communication will tend to flow more easily if you find an activity you can enjoy together as a starting point.

How would communication skills help Tracey? Where do her pictures of herself and her world come into a two-way process of discussion and negotiation? They come into it to the extent that you (or somebody) can discover them and help her to realize them.

- By playing peep-bo and making her laugh, you help her to discover that she can feel delight.
- By helping her to reach for things she wants, you can help her to discover that she can take an active part in her world.
- By being involved with her, you help her to discover that she is valued.

Such positive discoveries may be slow, but they can take place.

You may also become aware of her needs as a person without any power over her world. There may be many worrying and unpredictable happenings that she is not able to make sense of. Pain and confusion are things which make it hard for her to work out what she can do – leading perhaps to a sense of helplessness. Can you think yourself into Tracey's world and see through her eyes? We can assume and question but can we ever truly know another human being? Putting yourself in another's shoes is part of communication and depends on your relationship with them.

Debbie — seeing it through her eyes

'Debbie is four years old, blind and mentally handicapped. She seems to gain pleasure from poking her fingers deep into the sockets of her eyes. As a result she often gets eye infections. Thinking ourselves into Debbie's world begins with darkness – a world without light. She can't see what there is to play with and she bumps herself when she tries to explore. She will need a lot of help to find anything more interesting than the flashes of light she "sees" when she pokes at her eyes. She is also not aware that poking leads to infection.'
(From Newson and Hipgrave, 1982.)

Empathy with Tracey, or anyone else, begins with:
- seeing her as a person of worth with potential and places to go, worth working for and getting to
- believing that she has her own picture of herself and her world
- retaining an open mind by realizing that guesses may be wrong, but that they do provide a basis for thinking about new possibilities

A picture of the world

'One day Charlie had been asked to come to the hospital to "see if he could help a young man who wanted to paint". On this occasion the young man wasn't there, so there didn't seem to be a use for the perspex screen the workshop had made for finger-painting.

Not a use, that was, until a young 22-year-old who had been watching began to make noises. Julie has been wheelchair-bound all her life and doesn't speak, but Charlie thought she was trying to capture his attention. "Don't worry," said a member of staff, "Julie's always like that." But Charlie had a feeling that Julie was attempting to communicate with him. Accordingly he slowly approached and talked to her about the screen. Having asked her if she would like to paint, Charlie concluded, from Julie's movements and sounds, that she wanted to.

The following day he arranged for the perspex screen to be fitted to Julie's wheelchair. It was a nice day so they then placed her in the grounds, but were able to watch her from an office close by. Evidently, when Julie realised that she was on her own she, in Charlie's words, "opened up like a flower". "It was magic to watch," Charlie commented.

Julie then totally surprised her watchers. She fingered the paints, began to roughly mix them and soon was finger-painting on the perspex. Eventually Charlie, who had come out by then, noticed that Julie was clearly portraying the countryside scene that she could observe through the plastic. *But* in the middle was a RED SPOT. Intrigued, Charlie looked through the screen, and a long way away, was a red-roofed house.

Charlie had kept an open mind and discovered that Julie had a far more developed "picture of her world" than anyone had imagined.'

(From an account by Peter Durrant for the Campaign for Mentally Handicapped People in *CMH Newsletter*, No. 44, 1986.)

Other ways of communicating

For some people with a mental handicap and the key people in their lives, assessment is frustrated by the absence of any language. The use of alternative systems of communication, such as British Sign Language, has been an avenue to levels of communication that had not been thought possible.

Katie

'Katie is a three-year-old child with Down's Syndrome. She is the youngest of three children in the family. She seems to understand some of the things that are said to her, but her speech has not developed. Her parents say that there is some consistency in the sound she makes, but though they sometimes understand her "words" no one else does. She is a bright and active child who relates well with others and has a lot to "say" without words. Her parents think that she has difficulties with her hearing, but it is a problem which seems to come and go and a formal hearing test did not find anything.

Katie was introduced to an "alternative" system of communication using signs. The relief for the family and for Katie has been tremendous. They hadn't realized quite how frustrating the lack of communication was until they experienced the change.'

DON'T WORRY. HE'S ALRIGHT REALLY. HE JUST CAN'T COMMUNICATE VERY WELL

Various systems exist. The alternatives are described in the information box 'Alternatives to Speech', but any decision about using such a system and how to introduce it has to be taken carefully.

● What are the aims of using an alternative system? Is it being used to help Katie develop speech, for instance, or is it to be used instead of speech?

- Which alternative system would be best for this particular person? Should Katie, for instance, be introduced to the British Sign Language or to Paget-Gorman?
- Who else will master the system? Katie's parents would need to learn the system. What about the other two children in the family; will they learn the system? What about teachers, or friends?

Alternatives to speech

We can only give a very brief summary of some alternatives here. The book by Kiernan, Jordan and Saunders (1978) provides a fuller practical guide, and a book by Kiernan, Reid and Jones (1982) provides a more in-depth study.

1 *Sign languages.* These are natural languages which have been developed over the centuries by deaf people themselves. The British Sign Language has its own grammar which is very different from the English language. It is a communication system based on signs (and finger-spelling). The Makaton Vocabulary has been widely used to teach British Sign Language to people with a mental handicap. This is a vocabulary of about 350 signs which are presented in nine stages of 35–40 words. However, the strict use of the Makaton Vocabulary is open to question. The evidence suggests that it can be more helpful to introduce words as they become relevant to the child's needs and interests.

2 *Sign systems.* These are manual systems which are based on spoken languages. The best-known and most widely used is the Paget-Gorman sign system, which tries exactly to reflect spoken English. This differs from a 'sign language' in that it is a one-to-one sign-for-word system which allows for tenses, plurals and so on. The idea behind it is to provide an easier path for those who may develop spoken language later.

3 *Representational system.* The Bliss symbol system is one such system which has been used with children with severe learning difficulties. This is a language of line drawings which can be represented on cards, or boards. Usually a vocabulary of symbols is fixed on a board and the message is explained by pointing to the symbols in turn, e.g. for drink or food. One advantage is that the symbols have the words written underneath, so that even people not familiar with Bliss can talk with the Bliss user.

Signs and symbols should always be accompanied by normal grammatical speech.

Life histories

Communication skills and techniques are only a part of how people come to understand each other. They can help with building up and exploring the pictures people hold in their minds, but understanding somebody may involve knowing more about the wider context in which he or she lives. You may, as a parent, know all about your son or daughter's life history, but you may not know how he or she understands and interprets it. If you are not a parent, there are likely to be whole areas where you have no knowledge. Perhaps both you and your partner can make more sense of how you interpret and assess what is happening if you explore a bit of the past.

Richard

'Richard's teacher was having problems with his behaviour, which she described as "clinging" and "attention-seeking". He was ten years old at that time and did not get on with the other children in the class. Basically, he ignored them. All he seemed to want was his teacher's full and undivided attention. At first he just hung around her chatting, but the more she tried to get him to work and play on his own or with other children, the more his behaviour became "attention-seeking" such as tipping boxes of toys on to the floor. She felt stuck. None of her usual techniques worked.

What the teacher chose to do was a "My Book" project with Richard. (In fact, she had a project with the whole class but went a great deal further with Richard.) She became, in a way, Richard's biographer and compiled a *life history*. The book consisted mainly of photographs and pictures of people and places. Finding out about Richard and helping Richard find out about himself led to many important discoveries. His father had recently died, it emerged, and he needed help to make sense of what had happened to his life.

- She began with a "this is me now" part of the project, with photographs of himself and other members of his family.

(continued)

- She got in touch with his mother who also became interested in the project and supplied some photographs.
- The hostel where he stayed occasionally was also contacted and the teacher went along with Richard and took photos of the building and the care staff.
- Eventually she was able to use the book as a basis for discussions with Richard. He was able to talk about the hostel and what he felt about staying there, and about his father whose sudden disappearance had so disturbed him.'

SOME SPECIFIC ASSESSMENT TECHNIQUES

So far in our discussions about assessment we have been looking at the general two-way process of communication and how this can be improved. However, there can be times when assessment needs to be clearly focused on details to help towards a specific goal. Assessment is necessary to:

Establish existing abilities in order to plan
This is the best way of approaching a new task. For example, if your partner wants to learn to cook a simple snack, it will be important for you both to discover what his or her existing abilities are.

Discover factors which may contribute to difficulties
Specific assessment techniques may be required if, for example, it seems that your partner may have a hearing impairment.

Establish a baseline for measuring progress
You may both be working hard, perhaps on dressing skills. Complete independence in dressing may be a long way off, but having a baseline – a carefully measured account of how things were when you started out – can be invaluable for you both to show that progress is being made.

The techniques we shall look at are:

- observation
- checklists and scales
- formal assessment techniques

Observation

Observation techniques involve watching ourselves or others and taking note of actions or events. It varies from the open-ended approach of 'being together' to the sort of detailed methods such as the one described in the information box below. ABC observation has been used, for instance, by people who wish to give up smoking. They find out first exactly how many cigarettes they smoke and when.

'ABC' Observation

This is a three-part observation. In this example, we are talking about a child who has been having severe temper tantrums.

What happens before
Antecedents
That is, the observation and recording of what happens before a temper tantrum. This can include the general situation, such as the time when the child is angry and so on, as well as more specific events, such as a favourite toy being taken from the child.

What exactly does he or she do?
Behaviour
That is, the observation and recording of what exactly the child does; the child's actual behaviour. So, you would not record that the child had a 'temper tantrum', but rather that he or she screamed, pulled at his or her hair and kicked, for example. You would also record, for instance, the number of times he or she does these things.

What happens after?
Consequences
That is, the observation and recording of what happens after this behaviour. An obvious example here might be that he or she is shouted at, other activity in the room ceases, and so on.
  The approach is often called the 'ABC' for short.

Can you think of any time you might use the ABC approach? It might have helped to discover more about Tracey's screaming, for example. An ABC observation could tell us how often she has these periods and how long they last. It would also show us whether there was any sort of pattern in the time and circumstances when they occur, or in what is happening immediately after.

Activity

Think of some incident which occurs frequently in your household or workplace:

- rows
- someone losing his or her temper
- getting upset
- sulking

It could be anyone: yourself, another adult, a child, or you could choose someone with a mental handicap to focus on.

Try out the ABC. Next time it happens, write down as quickly as you can:

ANTECEDENTS
- What was happening?

- Who said what?

- What seemed to lead up to it?

- When did you notice it beginning?

- What time of day was it?

BEHAVIOUR
- What happened?

- Who was involved?

- What did each person do exactly?

CONSEQUENCES
- Who did what to whom?

- How did people feel and behave?

- How long did it last?

Sometimes, just this process of really paying attention and describing what happens leads to an understanding of what is going on. It then becomes much easier to tackle the situation.

Scales or checklists

Related to observation are *scales* or *checklists* which give details of behaviour you might look for. You simply work through the list checking what somebody does or can do already. The following is a short extract from one such checklist taken from a book for parents by Newson and Hipgrave (1982).

'PLAY
1 Follows moving person with eyes.
2 Increases activity at sight of interesting object.
3 Fingers over reflection in mirror.
4 Plays peep-bo.
5 Looks for toy which has been dropped.'

Scales differ in the areas and ages of development covered. They also differ in their clarity and the detail they give.

Examples of scales

Developmental scales have often been developed as part of research projects on child development. Several have arisen out of work undertaken at the Hester Adrian Research Centre (The University, Manchester M13 9PL). This could be a useful source of information. Many have also been published in books, which makes them easy to get hold of. Some examples include:

- Cunningham, C. and Sloper, P. (1978) *Helping your Handicapped Baby*, Souvenir Press.

This contains a scale of normal development up to two years for use by parents. Items are scored Yes/No. It covers four areas: physical/motor, adaptive behaviour, personal/social, and communication.

- Whelan, E. and Speake, B. (1979) *Learning to Cope*, Souvenir Press.

This includes a developmental scale for assessing coping skills in adolescents with mental handicap. It is for use by parents and professional workers. Items are scored on a seven-point scale and cover four areas: self-help, interpersonal, social and vocational.

- Newson, E. and Hipgrave, T. (1982) *Getting through to your Handicapped Child*, Cambridge University Press.

This is a scale of normal development for children up to five years and is scored Yes/No. It covers six areas: large body movements, hand-eye co-ordination, communication, play, feeding, dressing.

Formal assessment

We have deliberately postponed talking about *formal* assessment until now, although many people would probably think first of the sort of formal tests used by professionals, such as IQ tests. There are many ways of making such a *formal assessment*. It can be useful to think of these techniques as tools, in the same way as the Shared Action Plan approach is a tool. They are designed to do a specific job and they will only help us to measure what they have been designed to measure. Like all tools, some are better than others at doing their job. Also, like all tools, they can be used well and provide useful information, but they can also be used poorly or misused.

Formal assessment techniques

Some examples
1 *Medical assessment*
(a) General observation, including case histories and physical examination
(b) Specific tests – laboratory and other tests – including such things as chromosome analysis
(c) Specific tests for vision and hearing

2 *Developmental and psychological assessment*
(a) Developmental tests can be used with younger children to give information about various areas of development, for example, the Griffiths Mental Development Scale.
(b) Specific tests and investigations can look at a specific area of development, for example, a speech therapist might assess language development using the Reynell Scales or a physiotherapist might examine motor development and patterns of movement.
(c) Tests of intellectual development, such as the IQ (Intelligence Quotient) tests including the Wechsler Intelligence Scale for Children.

Christine

'Christine was 20 when her parents were advised by the ATC to look elsewhere for a place for her. Her life had been like that almost from the start. At school and at home her behaviour had led to rejections and one move after another. She had gone in the end to a special boarding school and was now back at home and being, it seemed, as difficult as ever.

On first meeting her, she was quite striking by her grace and poise. Beautifully dressed, she would sit and answer questions politely and naturally, but at other times she would be unco-operative, rude and aggressive. Her parents felt she needed a more normal setting, a job and more responsibility. The ATC was a last resort, they felt, for her and for them, and she was capable of far more.

It certainly seemed that way to the psychologist who saw them at that time. School records all suggested a girl who was underachieving and could do more if only someone could find the key. The frustration was how normal she looked and how well she could behave. Why did she keep, it seemed, letting herself down – and letting her parents down?

The psychologist suggested a formal assessment, partly as an opportunity to get to know Christine better on her own. She co-operated well and seemed to enjoy the experience. But the results came as a surprise. A standard intelligence test, the Wechsler Intelligence

(continued)

Scale, had been used and the results suggested that Christine was far less able intellectually than her appearance and surface behaviour suggested. This had to be thought about carefully. Did it make sense? Was it likely to be accurate? What would such information mean to Christine's parents or Christine herself? Would it be helpful or harmful?

At a follow-up meeting with Christine and her parents it was all discussed and many things seemed to fall into place. Christine had many strengths and often tried very hard, but from her point of view it seemed that people always expected more of her than she could manage. In the end she always came unstuck and felt she had failed. It seemed to make sense to her and to her parents. No wonder she often became sulky and aggressive. But what did it mean for the future? What about her parents' feeling that the ATC was wrong for her? That too made sense. Christine did not like it there and could probably achieve more if some of her difficult behaviour could be resolved.

Further discussion with the ATC staff and a careers officer led to the suggestion of a two-year residential course linked to the aim of finding job placements at the end. If Christine's real limitations could be understood as well as her obvious strengths, maybe on a course like this she could stop feeling like a source of distress and frustration for everyone, and begin to feel proud of herself for once.

The formal assessment did not provide any pat answers, but it did in this case suggest some new ways of thinking about Christine and helping her and her family to consider where to go next.'

Help and hindrance from assessment procedures

If we ask 'How well can this young man see?', and devise assessment techniques which allow us to measure his eyesight compared with most people's eyesight, the answer will tell us about his eyesight. If we ask about the level of intelligence, the answer will tell us something about how he seems to cope with a variety of tasks compared with other people of the same age. This method of comparison is the usual starting point in the design of the kinds of test listed above. The answers they give to such questions are not always as reliable as we would like, but they give an indication which is better than guesswork.

Formal assessment can provide a basis for dialogue between professionals, people with a mental handicap and the key people in their lives. But formal assessments can depend on the sort of understanding and mutual sensitivity which professionals might not have with a person who is mentally handicapped. Even apparently clear-cut tests depend on making personal judgements about whether someone is, or is not, reading, attending, distracted, in pain, relaxed and so on. They can become much more meaningful and helpful when they are part of a dialogue between the professional, the person with a mental handicap and somebody who knows them well. They can discuss questions such as:

- How happy are you with the assessment?
- How much faith would you put in these results?
- What do you think the implications of these results are?
- How do these results relate to what we know already?

These were the questions discussed with Christine and her family which helped them all to make sense of the assessment results.

Activity

Think about how *you* are, or might be, involved in using some of these processes with your partner in the Shared Action Plan. How might they help you both and are there any dangers you would watch out for?

HOW ASSESSMENT PROCESSES MIGHT HELP YOU AND YOUR PARTNER

ANY DANGERS YOU WOULD WATCH OUT FOR IN USING THESE ASSESSMENT PROCESSES

You may have some specific ideas arising from your particular situation, but here are some more general thoughts.

Ways that assessment processes might help
- They can help the process of communication, help you to get to know each other better, and develop your relationship.
- They can offer information which you may be able to use directly in planning ways of attaining goals.
- They may help you to review progress by providing a measure of how things are now against which progress can be measured.

Dangers you might watch out for

- Assessment processes can become ends in themselves rather than a means to an end. Professionals, for instance, can sometimes get stuck in a rut or cornered into churning out assessment results as a matter of routine. Checklists, too, can become 'cookbooks' which limit possibilities and imagination.
- Limitations in design may not be known and may create problems. For example, important steps can be missed out of checklists.
- There is the danger that they can be *done to* the person with a mental handicap rather than by or with him or her.
- These approaches are limited in their scope. They are focusing only on understanding the individual and do not help you both to measure, understand or make judgements about the attitudes of other people or the quality of opportunities available.

POSITIVE FACTORS AND DIFFICULTIES

Please now remind yourself of the guidelines for Form C, in section 4.3 of the 'Forms and Guidelines' appendix, and look again at the form itself. You are asked first to think about 'positive factors'. One approach to this is to focus on a person's strengths. This can help to direct attention positively on possibilities rather than negatively on what a person is not able to do and on problems. One of Michael Knight's goals, as you have seen, is to buy and learn how to ride a moped. As a young man just having left the sheltered world of a Special School for children with severe learning difficulties, he is likely to run into opposition for all kinds of 'good reasons'. His foster parents were alarmed when he wanted it on his Shared Action Plan. When they thought on the positive side and emphasized his strengths, they came round to seeing a different picture.

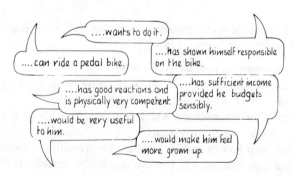

Thinking of strengths can help everybody – it makes you feel good and sets a positive optimistic tone. Parents often despair of assessment procedures which seem only to highlight the difficulties and to miss completely some of the good qualities their child has. When you think of strengths, you can open the door to seeing many positive characteristics you never saw before.

Nevertheless, focusing on a person's strengths can still be limiting, as we are only looking at the individual. Positive factors can also include the strengths of other people and good opportunities for the person to reach his or her goals.

If we return to Michael and the moped, for instance, people could think of lots of other 'positive factors'.

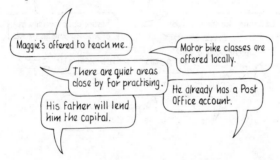

> Maggie's offered to teach me.

> There are quiet areas close by for practising.

> His father will lend him the capital.

> Motor bike classes are offered locally.

> He already has a Post Office account.

Remind yourself now about *your* Shared Action Plan Goals on Form B and agree with your partner on which one you will focus on for now.

Activity

Before you complete Form C, jot down some notes to work out what you might want to include on the form. Remember to do this with your partner.

What are the positive factors?
WHAT MIGHT HELP IN ACHIEVING THAT GOAL?

Remember to think about:

- your partner's strengths
- your own strengths
- other people's strengths

Remember that

● feelings, attitudes and circumstances are as important as abilities

Remember to consider:

● any existing services
● any existing opportunities

When they thought about the difficulties concerning this goal, Michael, Peter and Beth were still thinking positively. That is, they were already trying to think of things that must happen if this goal is to be achieved.

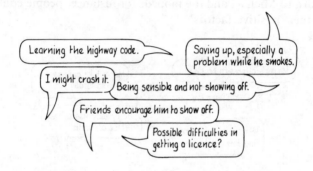

Learning the highway code.

Saving up, especially a problem while he smokes.

I might crash it.

Being sensible and not showing off.

Friends encourage him to show off.

Possible difficulties in getting a licence?

Activity

Think about any difficulties
WHAT FACTORS MIGHT CAUSE PROBLEMS?

Remember to think about:

● difficulties your partner may have
● difficulties you may have
● difficulties other people may have

Remember that

● feelings, attitudes and circumstances can cause difficulty, as well as lack of ability

Remember to consider:

- the lack of services
- the lack of opportunities

You have probably found that there were many points you could make here, even without taking more time to become involved in further assessment processes. Gathering further information and, for example, collecting together opinions or assessment results from other people are only likely to occur if Shared Action Planning is happening as part of your procedures at work. Parents on their own may find it hard, even these days, to get access to reports on their own relatives which they can incorporate here.

Look back now at the points you have made and check:

- Did you manage to find a way of involving your partner in this process?
- Did you include feelings, attitudes, and circumstances as well as abilities?
- Did you comment on yourself and others as well as your partner?
- Were there any difficulties of interpretation – for example, is 'knowing his own mind' a strength, or is it really 'stubbornness' and therefore a difficulty? Different viewpoints like this can help you to talk through and understand the issues better. Look back and underline any statements like this which could be interpreted differently.
- Are there further questions that have emerged which you would want time to go into. If so, make a note of them as 'Questions to be answered'.

At this point you are ready to transfer this information on to Form C. Please do that now.

Now you have worked through this chapter, you and your partner should be constructing a fairly well-documented account of the process that you are going through. You will probably also be aware that this process is *not* just about filling in the forms. It's a process of partnership; with discussion, shared experiences, observation and negotiation at the heart of it. Beth and Peter Hawkes felt that that was the case. They found it was the apparent 'spin-offs' that counted:

- the time spent together
- the risks they took in talking about things they might not have dared to raise otherwise
- the trust that developed as Mike began to believe in things that were written down

- the development in his sense of responsibility as he realized he was being taken seriously
- most of all, the development in their communication and awareness of relationships between them

Assessment, too, is bound up in the whole process. We have considered 'Assessment' in Chapter 3, *after* 'relationships' and 'aims and goals' but *before* 'action' and 'strategies'. But, as you have seen, it cannot really be seen separately like that. It has at least a double function. It is part of deciding on goals, and it's part, too, of putting plans into practice. So, for instance, for Katie and Richard assessment became the *action*. For Katie, the action was being introduced to an alternative system of communication and for Richard it was a life history. This is not unusual. It is quite common, for instance, for a person's behaviour to change while an ABC observation is being undertaken. Perhaps the extra attention and interest in the person was the action required. Perhaps things are changing between you and your partner as you go through the action of studying this workbook and making assessments together.

CHAPTER 4
SCHEMES OF ACTION: HOW TO PLAN FOR REACHING GOALS

First you worked out with your partner what you want to see happening. You have also thought about the positive factors which can help to achieve your goals – and the difficulties you will have to get around.

WHAT NEEDS TO HAPPEN NOW?

This section will be about answering the question 'What needs to happen now?' Sometimes answers will be obvious, and a range of possible 'action plans' will be in your head already when you reach this point. Then it can be easy just to note down what needs to happen. For example:

- keep working on the life history book together
- find someone for your partner to go swimming with
- teach your partner to make a cup of coffee
- invite a friend to tea

As long as there are no unexpected difficulties and you have the time and energy, then all kinds of simple plans can be set in motion. The extra nudge from having talked it all through and deciding what to try may be all that is needed.

Activity

Jot down some ideas you and your partner (and other key people if appropriate) can agree on about 'what needs to happen' to achieve one of your goals. First write down one of your aims and one of the goals which arose from that. Then add your ideas gradually. You may want to make changes or additions as you work through this chapter.

AIM   GOAL   WHAT NEEDS TO HAPPEN

It's not always easy. People may try all kinds of sensible ideas and still find they don't work out. They can end up feeling quite hopeless about making any changes.

This is when being more detailed about answering the question 'What needs to happen?' can really help. This is the stage when some careful 'action planning' can make all the difference. But what does careful or detailed planning involve? It means:

- considering your ideas carefully about 'what needs to happen'
- paying attention to details – 'dotting the '*i*'s and crossing the '*t*'s' on your plan
- sharing ideas and seeking support and advice from more people

CONSIDERING YOUR IDEAS

When you thought about aims and goals, you thought about *values* and how important it can be to look for goals which are valued in society. Now you have to remember to think about *valued means*, that is, ways or means of achieving goals which will themselves be valued. Are the suggestions you have written down likely to be valued?

Taking part in ordinary life experiences is valued, and shared planning emphasizes the need to pay attention to the two-way nature of this process. Shared Action Planning is not about one goal or a set of goals; it is about a process, a two-way process. It is about interacting with people, sharing experiences and learning about ordinary things. It is this interaction, this process of establishing a two-way flow of experience, which should form the heart of Shared Action Planning. Do your ideas include suggestions that will encourage a two-way process?

When you thought about positive factors and difficulties in Chapter 3, you tried to include information about circumstances and other people as well as about your partner as an individual. You can make use of that thinking now in considering your range of ideas. We now show you some ideas of other people using this approach to illustrate the point that things that 'need to happen' might focus on different issues.

Mary and Bob focused on Mary's *circumstances*. Mary lives in hospital and attends an Adult Training Centre daily. Bob is an instructor at the centre and on using this approach suggested:

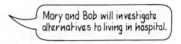

Gillian and her mother, with this approach, focused on an *interaction*, a relationship to support the interaction between Gillian and the opportunities around her.

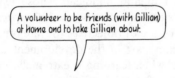

In Michael Knight's plan with his foster family, the focus was on his *individual development*.

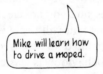

Do some of your ideas focus on different concerns?

PAYING ATTENTION TO DETAILS

The second aspect of careful planning is to think about the details of any suggestion. One way of doing this is to keep asking questions about how something will happen. For example:

Mary and Bob say they will investigate alternatives to living in hospital. You could have an imaginary conversation with them.

You   How are you going to do that?

Mary and Bob   Well, um, I think there's a hostel open and there might be
                 another opening soon, and we know some trainees at the
                 ATC live in a flat together – so we can ask about it.
You   Who will you ask?
Mary and Bob   Probably the social worker first.
Bob   I'll give him a ring.
You   Will you do that yourself, without Mary, do you mean?
Mary   I should be there. We should see him. I don't like phones.

And so on. They will have to work out when, who and what is involved in the simple process of investigating alternatives.

Can you add details to your ideas on page 70 to indicate *exactly who* needs to do *exactly what* and *exactly when*?

Objectives

For some people with mental handicap whose learning difficulties are severe, there may be a need to become even more specific: to think as well in terms of *objectives*. The use of objectives to state precisely what is intended has played an important part in the development of our ability to teach skills to people – even when learning is extremely hard for them.

Objectives tend to refer to immediate intentions; something to be achieved over the next few weeks, for example, or even the next few days.

● Clear objectives will improve your chances of reaching your goal.
● Stating objectives makes sure you are clear and precise about what you want to achieve and how you will achieve it.
● Objectives are usually stated in terms of behaviour – behavioural objectives – because behaviour is easier to see and describe than thoughts and feelings are.
● Objectives should be achievable in a short time-scale.

A behavioural objective states what a person will *do* or *be able to do* in clear, precise and measurable terms. *Do* is the key word here in that it must be observable behaviour. No 'fuzzies' are allowed. Thus, behavioural objectives begin by specifying:

Who will do what?
Michael Knight, for instance, wants to learn to drive a moped. That is a complex process, with many different skills involved. If he is to succeed, it may be necessary to think carefully about setting objectives which he can achieve one at a time. He can ride a pedal bike, but managing a heavier machine is quite different. A first objective might be to do with wheeling it

in and out of the garage and getting on and off the machine without letting it fall.

Under what conditions
He will need help and encouragement to start with and we know from him that Maggie has offered to teach him. He will also need fairly regular opportunities to practise. People learn best with short, frequent practising. So maybe the conditions should include help and advice from Maggie at least three times a week.

With what degree of success?
How will Maggie and Michael know when this first objective has been achieved? Managing once to manoeuvre the moped in and out and get on and off without it falling may not be enough if he dropped it the first time he tried, and scratched the car the second. Maybe three successful attempts in a row would be a good target to set, and might be achieved within a week if he tries it several times during each practice session.

The first detailed objective would then be: Michael will take his bike out of the garage, get on and off it, and return it to the garage, with help from Maggie, at least three times a week, until he has managed it three times without dropping it or bumping anything.

Long and detailed, but an objective like this will greatly increase his chances of success at the task. He and Maggie can then move on to next week's objective. For a more detailed discussion of using a behavioural approach, you could refer to the account by Blunden and Revill (1980).

Activity

Rewrite statements (a) to (d) so that they are behavioural objectives. You will find in each case that one of the four essential points is deliberately missed out or is not clear.

Remember the four essential points are (1) who, (2) will do what, (3) under what conditions, (4) to what degree of success.

Statements
(a) Anne will put on her shoes every morning.
(b) Brian will press the channel button for his favourite TV programme with a verbal prompt from his mother.
(c) Colin will know the value of coins up to £1, without prompts, correctly every time.
(d) Jane will be able to describe two methods of birth control accurately.

REWRITES
(a)

(b)

(c)

(d)

Missing essential point

(a) It does not specify 'under what conditions' so you might have added, for instance, 'without help'. Also the behaviour specified is somewhat imprecise and you might have added, 'and tie her shoe laces'.

(b) This objective does not specify 'to what degree of success', so you might have added, say, 'one programme per evening'.

(c) The verb *know* is not a behavioural verb. So you could have substituted *will name*.

(d) There is no 'under what conditions' here, so you might have added, 'without reminders when asked by her teacher'.

How did you get on? One person who tried it said it was a bit like doing mental arithmetic, but useful all the same. Behavioural objectives have been widely used and have brought about some remarkable advances in what individuals have been able to achieve. Objectives focus on the individual, but tend to draw attention to other changes that are needed. The story of Belinda provides an example of how starting with behavioural objectives led to a recognition of the need for wider changes.

Belinda: objectives as a starting point

'Belinda was 10 and had been living in a hospital ward for two years when the young psychologist first met her. As a part of his professional training, he was going to carry out a project in the hospital looking for ways to help some of the children there. Belinda was brought to his attention by the nursing staff and also by the psychiatrist in charge of the hospital. She sat silently in a corner and he might well not have noticed her at all. A closer look revealed a small child who would not look at him (or didn't notice him) with bald patches over most of her head, and what seemed, incredibly, like half of a bed sheet stuffed in her mouth.

"She keeps getting worse," he was told. "She won't do anything or join in anything now." She had started pulling her hair out about six months before, and stuffing her mouth had developed from mouthing and sucking things to packing her mouth full of any material she could lay her hands on...

Four months later, this same Belinda was laughing and dancing at her birthday party, her mouth empty and her hair regrown.

(continued)

How had it happened?

The answer was not, of course, easy, and it could never be complete, but it started with a simple plan of action that turned out to be not so simple and in the end spread ripples throughout the hospital.

First of all Belinda needed to be weaned off the large sheets packing her mouth, to smaller pieces of material and eventually to a dummy. She also needed distraction, and effective stimulation and interest to wean her away from hair pulling.

But to arrive at achievable objectives, she needed nursing staff who could get to know her, become involved in the details of the programme and spend time with her consistently over several months.

As things were that was not possible, but the nurses wanted to make it possible. The nursing officer became involved and changed shifts around, modified the student nurses' patterns of movement around the hospital, and they got things started.

But really Belinda needed more. She needed just a few staff she could get to know well, a smaller environment where she could be more easily involved in activities.

The plan of action grew and spread. The consultant and the hospital administrator became involved. That house in the grounds . . . perhaps if . . . what would need to happen? Staff organization? Food and cooking to be done in the house? Who else might live there? Costs?

It happened, and suddenly no one needed a detailed programme to get to know Belinda and keep her interested and involved. Relationships and involvements sprang up more easily in a setting where a small group of children could behave more naturally with each other. Giving her time and attention was easier now, especially as she too was becoming more outgoing and trusting.

The action plan had been essential as a focus to ask the questions and set the tasks, and perhaps the proof of success was in reaching the point where it became redundant. A new stage was reached and perhaps soon a new action plan would start to emerge. Already she was seeing the speech therapist. And in the meantime Belinda had remembered how to laugh and dance.'

Behavioural objectives can refer to *skills* and *actions*, but they are usually skill-based, that is, they state something an individual will be able to do after a period of learning. A review of the Individual Planning system

(Humphreys *et al.*, 1985) questions this emphasis. The evidence made them ask 'whether a system based on skill-teaching was appropriate for all clients, or for the solution of all needs'. A skill-based objective would oblige your partner to learn and to change, whereas it is possible that he or she might just want more opportunity to do something for pleasure, like playing football or going to the pictures.

Objectives can refer to a *product* or a *process* or an *experience*. Behavioural objectives, whether they involve new skills or not, are about achieving specific tasks. They are sometimes known as *product* objectives because they lead to a product. This use of product objectives has been helpful in developing teaching techniques and enabling people to learn things that we were not previously skilled enough to teach. But sometimes the focus on describable behaviour is restricting. We may hope that someone can learn to make friends, to find his or her way to a new address, or to plan a meal – in other words to understand and be able to apply a *process* in new situations. Such objectives are not strictly behavioural – they have been called *process* objectives (Further Education Unit, 1980), and they try to encompass the need for objectives which do more than concentrate on separate skills.

In education, another form of objective which can be useful is the *experiental* objective (see, for instance, Brennan, 1985). This form of objective refers to:

'situations designed to engage a person in a problem, experience or task, without specifying in advance what the particular learning/behavioural outcome might be.'

You might, for example, feel it would be valuable for someone to go swimming, without wanting to state precisely what that person should achieve as a result.

An example of the type of approach is provided by Atkinson and Ward (1986) in their discussion of possibilities of 'neighbourhood contacts'. Their recommendations imply experiential objectives, such as 'the person will have experience of, and be engaged in neighbourhood activities and contact'. This would involve the person choosing places to visit and activities in which to become engaged such as going to a pub, a club or swimming. He or she may require help to ensure that things go as smoothly as possible.

It is not the individual's behaviour or skills which are being focused on but a series of visits and activities that can be tackled jointly by that person and others involved. A major advantage of this type of approach is the emphasis on a shared process.

These differences often became very clear to people struggling with real plans to help real people. One community care worker described her early problems with setting objectives:

> 'We tried to teach Donna to open tins of food. It seemed right because she could begin to be independent, maybe get a meal herself and so on. Well, we'd been working on it for weeks and weeks before we discovered that her dad was horrified. We didn't know – but she would just go into the pantry and open tins. It was hopeless, you see, because it wasn't anything to do with real life for her – at that stage it didn't mean anything!'

What they learned was that people need to start by just taking part. Experiencing and discovering what it is about, and what the people are about, has to happen first. Then process objectives can emerge, suggesting how they might begin to master parts of the process for themselves. Only then, if real difficulties are encountered with a particular skill that seems hard to acquire, may a precise product objective be appropriate and necessary.

If necessary, you might want now to rephrase some of your statements on page 70 about what needs to happen as clearly stated objectives. If particular skills that may be hard to learn are involved, you might want to seek some professional advice. This is what we turn to next.

SHARING IDEAS

Many different skills may be called for in a Shared Action Plan, and this can sometimes require a group of people working together, each knowing what the other is doing. Have a look at the guidelines in section 4.4 and at Form D itself in the 'Forms and Guidelines' appendix, and then look again at your ideas for what needs to happen. Does there seem to be an advantage in bringing in some other people before Form D is completed?

If other people are to be involved you may want to think about whether this can just involve seeking advice, maybe arranging an appointment or a home visit; or whether it really calls for a more organized meeting because the provision of resources or services will have to be discussed and agreed. If there is a key worker involved, his or her advice should be particularly valuable at this point.

The Individual Programme Plan system has tended to require large meetings. In their review, however, Humphries and others (1985) found:

'Of all the participants at Individual Programme Planning meetings, clients themselves contributed least . . . clients felt least happy with opportunities for being able to express their opinions at the meetings.'

A parent said of such meetings:

'She felt manoeuvered a bit, all these people sorting out her next step.'

Another said:

'He was upset for weeks after.'

The regular meetings can cause problems for the professionals too, who find themselves expected to attend every one that takes place – an impossible task for them.

In Shared Action Planning these problems have been taken account of as far as possible by:

- having small groups of two or three people to take things as far as possible, with a larger meeting only called if necessary
- having a place on Form B: Overall Aims and Directions to record the views of the person with a mental handicap
- allowing for the possibility of having a small informal meeting of key people even at Form D stage, if that seems to be what is wanted
- strengthening the contribution and responsibility of the individual, the family, and any care staff involved by helping them to develop their ideas on paper *before* any discussion or larger meeting with professionals or service managers

Now you have considered your ideas about what needs to happen in terms of:

- what they focus on
- how detailed they are
- whether further advice or support is necessary

Activity

It is time to summarize your starting points on Form D
Fill in your aim, goal, what needs to happen and who is to be responsible. If further advice is needed or a meeting should really be held, make a note of that as an action plan. Who might you contact to see if it would be possible?

This has been a carefully thought-through process which will have taken you some considerable time. It was interesting to us that although some people who looked at the forms thought they might be too difficult for people to fill in (would parents be able to cope – or care staff?), the readers who did use them were often quite happy and certainly seemed to have filled them with interesting and thoughtful comments and ideas. They felt they *were* useful for various reasons.

Because so many people are involved and there is a risk of communication breaking down.

By keeping records it is easier to see if the action has been successful.

In some circumstances the plan can act as a form of contract so that everyone knows what part they must play.

Beth, Michael's foster mother, felt at the start that it was 'a bit like finding my way through a computer manual'. Michael himself decided the forms were 'rubbish', but he became very upset and indignant when they thought they had got lost one evening.

People seldom love forms for their own sake and we would not want that to happen here. What the forms do is to help to give structure to a process – a process of developing relationships and ideas in partnership, and a process that you are by now, we hope, fully engaged in.

With that in mind, Chapter 5 is designed to help you explore a range of possibilities for Shared Action Plans.

CHAPTER 5
ACTION TACTICS: WAYS OF PUTTING PLANS INTO PRACTICE

Once a journey of change has been embarked upon, it is time to turn the plans into actions. In Chapter 4 we suggested that planning needs to focus on action in three ways: circumstances, interactions and individual development. You and your partner will therefore have thought about various ways of moving forward towards your aims and goals. Sometimes one idea will work, sometimes another. Sometimes more than one will be needed. Sometimes you may find yourselves stuck on one track which does not seem to be working. In this chapter you will have a chance to consider a whole range of possibilities which may give you both some new ideas.

- We begin by looking outwards from the individual's point of view to *circumstances and other people*.
- We then concentrate on the *interaction* between the individual and those other people and opportunities in the environment.
- And finally we look at *individual development* and possible ways of supporting learning.

We hope that you will find these three ways of looking at things helpful, but we do not wish to pretend that they are totally separate and entirely different from each other. At heart, which ever way you look, you will see *relationships* between one person and another and the two-way flow of *communication* between them.

Planning can be a long and at times painful process because it is a matter of weighing up priorities. If you spend time and energy on one thing, you inevitably have less for something else. Chapter 5 is about some of the possible priorities that you and your partner may choose. When you have read this chapter, we shall ask you to return to your Shared Action Plan and think again about possibilities for action.

CIRCUMSTANCES AND OTHER PEOPLE

What you see depends on where you are looking from. What happens if you try to look at the physical and social world from the perspective of people with a mental handicap? This involves you in looking outwards from the individuals to *their* lives and experiences, and to the circumstances and other people as *they* see them.

(Based on ideas in an Open University unit on disability [1982].)

The first thing that happens is that you become in a sense the outsider to this way of looking. Who knows what it means to be 'mentally handicapped'? Only people with a mental handicap can speak from the real experience of their daily lives and of the attitudes and behaviour of others towards them. This then must be the starting point: to understand what is needed from the point of view of people with mental handicap speaking on behalf of themselves. This focus, then, involves people who are mentally handicapped speaking up for themselves. Sometimes it can be in 'self-advocacy groups', such as the trainee committees or student councils emerging in Adult Training Centres and Social Education Centres.

Self-advocacy involves individuals learning to believe in themselves and their rights. In its most basic form people are becoming their own advocates whenever they express *their* views, feelings or wishes to others in whatever way they find most effective. Yet such seemingly simple beginnings can really make you think again about how you do things.

Perhaps the first fundamental challenge has been to the label of 'mental handicap'. This comes in many forms. The president of the 'People First' self-advocacy group in London, for instance, opened the conference to mark their first anniversary as follows:

> 'It's an organization for people who are self-advocates and who want to speak up for their rights and put new ideas forward and have a better position. It's for people who've been labelled "mentally handicapped", though we don't like that word.'

This challenge is becoming widespread now. Increasingly the term *learning difficulties* is being used within self-advocacy groups and in other settings. We were roundly condemned by one person, who would accept that she had learning diffculties but completely rejected our use of the term *mental handicap*. We failed that particular challenge at the time for what seemed like all kind of good reasons to us, but maybe *you* will accept the challenge.

There is a change too in the personal experience of having a 'mental handicap'. Self-advocacy groups, for instance, foster a change in attitude. They can offer feelings of security and confidence, a kind of 'psychological safety'. This is a good basis for the growth of self-respect. Speaking for people with physical disabilities, Allan Sutherland (1981) puts it this way: 'We are not weak; we are not powerless, we are not alone. Control of our future is ours for the taking.'

Ultimately the challenge is to our understanding of the term *mental handicap*. From the individual's perspective the problem is not so much the difficulties with learning, the struggles to acquire social skills, or the medical explanations for their problems. The problems *they see* are the difficulties and obstacles people put in their way; the experiences, opportunities (or lack of them), attitudes and conditions of society they have to face as a result of being labelled 'mentally handicapped'.

Do you and your partner see it this way too? Can you think, with him or her, about how to tackle such problems?

Activity

How can you support and help self-advocacy by people with a mental handicap? This focus must obviously have implications for the role of anyone wishing to be a helper. Following is a list of what self-advocacy might involve for your partner. Next to it please give a list of what you think this might mean for your role.

YOUR PARTNER	YOURSELF
1 Growth and confidence	
2 Trust	
3 Self-valuing/pride	
4 Identity	
5 Determination	
6 Responsibility	
7 Ability and knowledge	
8 Sensitivity to others	
9 Developing a voice	

Paul Williams and Bonnie Schoultz (1982) have written a book called *We Can Speak for Ourselves*. In it they suggest that serious thought needs to be given to the role of helper to self-advocacy groups. You may have used different terms, but perhaps some of the points you made overlap with some of their suggestions for the helper's role:

- enhancing mastery and control
- learning to be on their side in seeing problems
- learning to enjoy and know people
- believing in people
- commitment
- accentuating positive qualities
- sharing skills and information
- monitoring your own communication
- learning to assist without control or power

Another source of suggestions could be found in the video and training manual produced by D. Cooper and J. Hersov (1986) on self-advocacy.

These suggestions don't only apply to group situations. Some people found they had to learn these skills in a one-to-one relationship.

Remember Peter and Beth Hawkes with their foster son, Michael. Peter felt they were often falling into the trap of trying to wield the power – turning the procedure into a lecture. *Now* you see why you shouldn't smoke, should save money, etc. Those of you who are parents will know how easy that is. Can *you* learn instead to help someone towards his or her *own* thinking and to accept that maybe he or she won't reach the same conclusions as you.

Some questions can help people to think:

- How do you think you could . . .?
- What would you feel if . . .?
- Would you like to . . .?

So can open-minded suggestions, such as:

- Some people think that . . . .
- Or you could try . . . .
- I once had a problem like that and I tried . . . .
- What did 'so and so' do when that happened to him?

Tone of voice matters too, of course. Any questions can sound off-putting if they are not said genuinely. Stop and think again if you find yourself saying:

- What you should do is . . . .
- You really must try to . . . .
- Don't you think it would be best if . . .?

If your partner cannot speak or even understand language, it is harder to learn to do this. Questions about 'what might happen if' may be too complex, and the starting point will be with the simple choices, remembering that your partner may need time to choose.

- Will it be this jumper or that to wear today?
- Shall I have a drink just now or not?
- Shall I go out or stay in?

This has to be balanced, of course, against widening choices by encouraging your partner to try new things. This can mean:

- taking it slowly and not forcing or frightening him or her (e.g. with swimming or trying new food)
- watching other people trying it out – not insisting on joining in at once

- trying it again later on if it hasn't worked this time
- trying to make the new experience positive at the time and afterwards (e.g. a photograph of Mary at the seaside – 'Look, she put her toe in the sea!' rather than 'Mary was frightened; she wouldn't go in the water'.)

This question of the role played by the 'helper' arises in a number of ways when self-advocacy groups meet. A class called 'Speaking for Ourselves' meets with John Hersov every week at the City Lit in London and they often choose to discuss such matters. They have, for instance, talked about 'Key workers and social workers – where do we stand in relation to them?' and 'Would staff accept criticism?' Their relationship with people who

Would staff accept criticism?

offer help changes also when they decide as a group that they will choose to approach someone for help. This particular group, for instance, asked along someone from the DHSS to answer questions they had about Supplementary Benefit.

The members of the group have also spent time looking at how they can help each other gain confidence and skills, in leading discussion groups for instance. As they become stronger and more self-sufficient they are more and more able themselves to influence their relationship with helpers.

Perhaps at this point in our workbook we should respond to this greater strength and allow our 'helping' relationship to be influenced; we should listen also to our own arguments and respond to the challenge in our last activity. If we try to see it their way and look, with them, from their point of view, maybe then we will feel we have to tackle such problems – particularly the problem of the 'mental handicap' label. Perhaps we too should decide to adopt their preferred term of *learning difficulty*. There are no right answers to this. It will certainly lead to other complications and confusions of definition, and will clash with formal decisions on terminology in government acts and so on. But that will be nothing new and perhaps such a move on our part will speed up some further debate which has to take place sooner or later. It is a risk, but then any change involves some risk. So, from here on, we shall leave the term *mental handicap* behind and try to talk in terms of *learning difficulties* instead.

Support partnerships

You have been thinking, from your partner's point of view, about how circumstances and other people can change to allow more supportive relationships to develop. But what about the relationships between the supporters themselves?

Whatever your role in the Shared Action Planning, you are going to have a relationship not only with your partner but with others who can offer their contribution. This involves a different kind of partnership, such as those that can exist between parents and professionals or between teams of staff who work together. A good balance is difficult to achieve, as you may know from experience.

Your partnership in Shared Action Planning involves a two-way process of sharing and communication. Partnerships between supporters must also involve a *sharing* of what each has to offer, a sharing of knowledge, understanding and skills. A group of parents and carers met in a 'workshop' to discuss this process of sharing and spoke, in particular, of how they felt about their relationships with professionals. They started at a disadvantage, it seemed.

> All these people deal with you one at a time. But you have to cope with all of them.

Activity

The parents and carers made some suggestions to help build partnerships. Try to think of some suggestions from your own experiences. Jot down any attitude or approach you have found helpful in creating a good working partnership between parents or others with a close relationship on the one hand, and professionals, who are likely to be less frequent visitors, on the other hand. You can do this, even if your own role is a professional one.

YOUR SUGGESTIONS TO HELP BUILD PARTNERSHIPS

Suggestions from the workshop included:

- Parents and carers should have confidence in what they themselves have to offer.

  'It's simple. They must *earn* your respect as a parent. And you must believe in yourself.'

  'I can't tell people their jobs, but I'd like them to look at *me* as an expert. I've had 20 years' practical experience as a parent now.'

- Parents, or carers, may need to support each other in this partnerships with professionals.

  'His mother and I were both a bit worried about what was happening at the ATC. Anyway, we both went together to see them at the ATC. We sort of gave each other moral support.'

- A personal relationship can be of crucial importance.

  'It's the relationship you have with the professional that matters. It doesn't matter what label they have. It's what they are like as a person that matters.'

- Parents and carers must understand the constraints on professionals.

  'You've got to find a sympathetic professional, one you can get on with. But you must remember that professionals can't buck the system. The system pays them their salaries.'

- Parents and carers should speak out and make sure they are listened to.

  'Make your fears and doubts known. I *tell them*. Otherwise they'll just think everything's all right.'

  'You've got to "think on" when you want something done. You have to be ready. You have to have all your information ready. You must take notes, keep a diary of all that happens. Be ready.'

Similar points are made in the book by Newson and Hipgrave (1982) if you would like to read more about it.

Do some of these suggestions sound familiar? Building self-confidence; speaking out; gaining strength from each other: these were some of the same self-advocacy skills you thought about earlier on page 84. If you are a professional, maybe you found your suggestions were similar to the list of 'support skills' in that same activity.

Some practical suggestions came from our discussions with people using this approach:

Regular meetings
- visiting the home, the school, the hospital or the ATC on a regular basis
- meeting in neutral places such as the toy library
- meeting for a purpose, like discussions, a Shared Action Plan, reviewing progress, and so on

Improved communication
- perhaps through something like home-school diaries or regular reports or exchanges of notes
- keeping in touch by phone over minor things
- remembering to take it in turns to listen as well as to talk

Keeping in touch through a key worker
- somebody to liaise and make sure everyone knows what everybody else is doing and feeling

You might want to add that this wider partnership with professionals will only be successful from the point of view of your Shared Action Planning partner if he or she remains central to the picture.

INTERACTION

Your partner's Shared Action Plan goals are quite likely to involve some kind of interaction – with people, in social situations, or with practical arrangements like transport or shopping. Your partner may look to you for support in negotiating some of these interactions. You are not being asked to take over, but just to support the interaction, to help it to happen.

A word which describes this role is *mediation*. Mediation is not a completely new idea. You may be aware that it is something that you do a great deal in the course of your everyday life or job. You may mediate between your child and the irate owner of the broken window. You mediate if you explain a news item to somebody, or help someone to fill in a complex form.

Activity

Are you a mediator? Try to think of some times when your partner makes use of you to support an interaction. Now jot down a few examples.

EXAMPLES OF MEDIATION

Some good mediation examples offered to us are:

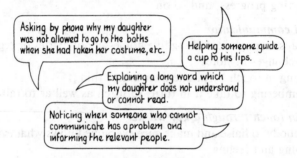

Another example of mediation which was described to us is summarized in the box entitled 'Liz – more than a listening ear'.

Liz – more than a listening ear

'Liz runs adult education classes, including some on self-advocacy. She also has an open door policy for any students who want to talk. Occasionally, it happens that someone will come in very upset. Liz offers that person support and a chance to talk and explain what has happened to him or her. Often the stories are complex and involved, and Liz writes down what she is told as the individual goes along – checking on details and helping the student to explain. Then she reads it back to him or her slowly and carefully. These students then

(continued)

know it is theirs because they hear their own words. It's what they wanted to say.

The paper with the story on it can now be theirs. If they prefer it to remain private for now, perhaps because the sharing alone has been enough, then it can be locked away for them and no one else will see it without their permission.

They can use it, however, and they often do, to show somebody else what has happened. It helps them to communicate more easily with other important people they wanted to tell, but couldn't. It acts as a very effective form of mediation.'

Perhaps you included some of the following examples:

- mediating information: for example, translating some instructions or a story into simpler language.
- mediating between people: for example, helping to sort out a misunderstanding; putting people at their ease to make communication possible; explaining someone else's intentions and wishes to someone
- mediating between somebody and a task: for example, guiding someone towards achieving a task that he or she is intent upon

One critical area for mediating between people is in encouraging relationships between people with learning difficulties and other members of the community. The next activity will help you to think about how you might do this.

Activity

You could start by making a list of *your own* opportunities for meeting and getting to know other people. Add to your list things you might do if you wanted to extend your opportunities.

MY OPPORTUNITIES FOR GETTING TO KNOW OTHER PEOPLE

IDEAS TO EXTEND MY OPPORTUNITIES IF I WANTED MORE

The question of developing opportunities was discussed at the

Conference on Informal Supports in America (1985). They produced a list of 'places to start' which we have summarized below. You might like to compare your ideas for *yourself* with their ideas for *themselves*.

1   Start with *other people.*

● Family, friends of the family, and care workers; these can represent a network of potentially hundreds of contacts for people with learning difficulties.

● People in the community who are willing and interested in taking the first step into a relationship with someone with learning difficulties. In some areas of the country there are schemes to find volunteers to befriend people with learning difficulties. (The story of Norma and Janet, which was described to us by Janet, shows how well this can work.)

The starting point, then, is you and the social network that you are part of. That is why we asked you to look at your own opportunities in the preceding Activity. On your list are the places and people which you as a mediator can or could offer.

2   Their next idea was *places and events* which can offer opportunities for people to meet and form relationships. Just the presence of individual people with learning difficulties at weddings, fairs, markets, churches, concert halls, and so on, can be a starting point.

3   Another suggestion they had was *organizations, common interests and activities* which help bring people together. These could include political organizations, adult education classes, weight-lifting, jogging and sporting activities of many kinds. From their work in Ireland, McConkey and McCormack (1983) also suggest that attitudes are more likely to change if people share joint activities in familiar situations.

Norma and Janet

'How can people with learning difficulties have a better chance of getting out and meeting people? This is the question which a befriending scheme in a city in the north of England is trying to answer. It was the community nurse who introduced Norma to the scheme. Norma was 34 at the time and lived with her father. They

(continued)

went out together on a Friday and Sunday evening to the club at the Community Centre where most of the people were more her father's age than Norma's. On Mondays she went to the club for the trainees at her ATC. Apart from these trips out, she sat at home with her father watching television. She saw the scheme as a chance to "go out as much as I can". Janet, on the other hand, became a befriender and met Norma because she saw it as a way of earning a bit of money, but at the same time "doing something worthwhile". She was training to become a teacher.

Norma and Janet became friends. At first they went where Norma wanted to go, that is to the same Community Centre as she went with her father. But then they "launched out". Norma liked music and dancing, so they started going to a local folk-music club and then they went to discos. They tried different places together: a day by the sea, a morning shopping, a visit to the cinema, a quiet evening in a pub and a barbecue at Janet's house. They would meet some of Janet's other friends when they were out.

There were difficulties to be overcome of course. From Janet's side there was the practical difficulty of just planning arrangements. It was difficult to get in touch with Norma and she kept breaking arrangements. Janet found that hard to take. She would make time to see Norma only to find that she had made other arrangements and was "totally unaware" of how that made Janet feel... There were physical difficulties: Norma has muscular dystrophy. Her hygiene and appearance also created difficulties. She had "accidents" and she smelt, but she didn't like Janet to fuss or get angry about her appearance or her weight or her forgetting a date, or anything else.

There was, of course, a positive side. Both simply got enjoyment out of their friendship. Both also developed a greater awareness and wider experience. Janet, who had no family living locally, found that a friend "helps you feel you do belong to a place". Norma was experiencing what young people do and seeing more people, many more people, than her closed circle had allowed.

This story has a sad ending. Norma was moved into a hostel as her father became increasingly unable to cope. There she developed a circle of new friends and doesn't seem to think she needs Janet any more. After 3–4 years of friendship and going out together Janet is missing Norma's company. She is hoping that at some time Norma will change her mind and want to go out with her again.'

To increase opportunities is often not enough however. There can be obstacles to friendly interaction with other people. Another workshop held by the same group of parents and carers described earlier was based on the theme of 'Coping in the Community'. They spoke first of some of the problems they had met being out and about in the community with a person with conspicuous learning difficulties, simply going places and meeting people. Here are just a few of the things they mentioned:

They say, 'What's wrong with him – is he crackers?,' just because my son uses Makaton.

Some say, 'isn't it a shame?'

And if you tap her for being naughty it's, 'How dare you smack a handicapped child?'

My son wanted to use the toilet, but we found the disabled loo was in the Ladies.

When we go on a train he has to go in the guard's van in his wheelchair. Where's the dignity in that?

K joins in the hymn singing. She sings ever so loud. It's so embarrassing.

It's the bride's day. They don't want it spoilt.

They don't want those kids on the photographs.

My grandmother would cross the street to avoid me. She thought I must be touched by the Devil to have had two handicapped children.

The minute my kids went out to play, the other kids were called in.

It's the long queues that make shopping so difficult.

They said on the phone I could open a bank account for her, but when we got there it was a different story.

Her friends outgrew her.

It was not all problems and 'We haven't found that' was perhaps the phrase most often used that evening. Also some parents found that the problems changed as their child grew older. Everyone, however, had encountered problems of some sort and some people had 'become more and more isolated'. So what can be done to cope with such difficulties? How do you, as a mediator, find yourself trying to ease the stress of interactions like these – to keep the door open for positive community interactions to develop?

Activity

The parents and carers at the workshop discussed the tactics they had found useful in dealing with the problems they encountered. In many ways it is like learning to be 'street-wise'. Before you read some of their suggestions, note down a few of your own ideas.

YOUR IDEAS OF TACTICS FOR DEALING WITH PROBLEMS

The group first of all agreed that the only real way to overcome these problems, in the end, was through properly organized integration.

The parents and carers had different approaches to tackling the problems. Some wanted to ignore or avoid the problems.

Others preferred a more direct approach – giving as good as they get:

'Giving as good as they get.'

Or turning the tables on them:

> When someone says,'I bet you have a lot
> to put up with', I often say,'Probably not
> as much as you!'

Others used a more educational approach:

> I invite them in so they can see what he can do.
> You have to explain to them that there are
> children who aren't like them.

And in relation to the practical problems they had some tips like:

> The TSB, building societies and
> the Post Office are good if you
> want to open an account.

> You can open an account
> in joint names.

> You can apply for a key of
> your own to disabled loos.

If they wanted help or advice in 'coping in the community', who would
they turn to? They were all in agreement about the answer to this:

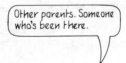

> Other parents. Someone
> who's been there.

For some people with learning difficulties the first question may be who will mediate on their behalf. Citizen advocates accept a formal role to mediate for somebody, to make sure that a person with learning difficulties is personally represented in matters which affect him or her directly. There are schemes such as the Advocacy Alliance (115 Golden Lane, London, EC1Y 0TJ) which was established in 1981 to recruit and train volunteers to act as advocates for long-stay hospital residents, and it plans to expand its work into the community as well.

You may have already been working on a Shared Action Plan which included an advocate to represent individuals with learning difficulties and to help them in putting their own views forward. Remember how Michael Knight and his foster parents brought in his ex-teacher to act as an advocate for Michael. They all found that helped a lot. The advocate was able to mediate and ease some of the conflict in the interactions between them.

In your partnership in Shared Action Planning, you will inevitably act as a mediator from time to time, explaining things, providing information, supporting new contacts and ideas, and aiding communication with other people. You may even be formally in the role of an advocate. There is no sharp dividing line. As a parent or carer your close relationship may make you the best mediator in many situations. There will be times, though, when you and your partner have different goals and interests to protect. Michael Knight wanted to protect his right to independence; Beth and Peter wanted to protect their input of time and affection as foster parents. Hence the clash they had over his goal of leaving home. At times like these an outside mediator may be necessary. Think about it yourself.

Your Shared Action Plan partnership should not become exclusive. The input of an additional, more detached point of view from an advocate who will support your interaction with each other need not threaten your own role. Rather it may help to strengthen your relationship.

INDIVIDUAL DEVELOPMENT

So far you have looked with your partner at influencing *circumstances* by changing how other people behave; you have looked at how you *mediate* between your partner and the circumstances or people around. Now you can both consider ways in which your partner could learn to do more for himself or herself.

Learning is an active process in which a person changes through experiences and interactions with others and with the world around him or her. Learning requires some change, a shift from set patterns or habits and comfortable assumptions and expectations. As in all change, there is an element of risk in the process of learning, not least being the risk of failure. You and your partner will want to consider this as you weigh up your priorities and decide on the approach you want to try first. There are three important points.

1   Learning is a two-way process

Think about the following brief description. Who is learning to do what?

A mother puts her daughter in her cot. The child cries loudly. The child is picked up by her mother and she stops crying.

The child is learning to cry when put in the cot, because when she cries something nice happens, that is, she gets picked up and cuddled. But the mother is also learning. She is learning to pick up her child when she cries, because when she does something nice happens to her too, the child stops crying. If this happens night after night, a pattern will be set up that can be very difficult to change.

2 Learning is part of everyday contact between people

As the example in point 1 shows, we influence each other's behaviour all the time. You can see this, too, in the three cartoon strips. They show how each child is learning through the interaction with their mother.

3 Teaching involves understanding how learning occurs

We all learn more effectively if we are taught well. If your partner's goals include learning something new, then it is important to understand how everyday interactions can help people to learn. Whether they knew it or not, the mothers in the cartoon were using a mixture of teaching techniques. They were also, of course, learning themselves, in becoming skilled at shopping successfully with a young child.

Techniques they were using

Positive reinforcement

That is, the child was rewarded for the behaviour by smiling approval from the mother, and by getting the yoghurt.

Breaking the task down

Choosing the yoghurt involved: finding it, finding a brand they like, choosing a flavour, deciding on size and putting it in the basket.

Demonstrating appropriate actions

The first mother was 'showing how', whilst helping the child to notice what she was doing and why.

Prompting appropriate actions

The middle child could complete the task of choosing the yoghurt himself with some prompts, in this case spoken reminders, from his mother. The third child had reached the stage of carrying out the task unaided, although he probably still needed his mother there to give him confidence.

Although the cartoon examples involved a child and mother, the techniques apply to us all.

You can look at these four 'techniques of teaching' in more detail. The first one, 'reinforcement', is to do with the *consequences* of someone's behaviour – what happens to him or her as a result.

Consequences of behaviour

Table 2 shows four types of consequence that can follow behaviour. The word *behaviour* here means any kind of action, from smiling to washing the car. It doesn't just mean good behaviour or bad behaviour.

Table 2   Four types of consequence

	Consequences which strengthen behaviour (i.e. they make it more likely to happen again)	Consequences which weaken behaviour (i.e. they make it less likely to happen again)
Things that are given	Positive reinforcement involves giving something nice, e.g. sweets, praise, a smile, a large strawberry yoghurt	Punishers which involve *giving something unpleasant*, e.g. slapping, shouting
Things that are taken away	Negative reinforcement involves stopping or taking away something unpleasant, e.g. stopping nagging, taking the frown off your face	Punishers which involve *taking away something pleasant*, e.g. favourite TV programme switched off, or no tea tonight

Activity

We have left spaces in Table 2 in which we would like you to write your own examples.

(a) In each of the four types of consequence write down first an example of consequences which might change your behaviour.

(b) Then do the same for your partner. That is, give an example which might change your partner's behaviour for each of the four types of consequences.

You might like to use different colour pens for (a) and (b).

It is important to remember that a reward for one person may not be pleasurable to another, and may even be a punisher: 'One person's meat is another person's poison.' For instance, praise is usually a pleasurable experience, but it does depend on who is praising whom.

Here are some examples we were given:

Positive reinforcement
'money'
'a hand in friendship'
'new record'
'being talked to'

Punishers (which involve giving)
'too much noise'
'getting thumped'
'starts screaming'

Negative reinforcement	*Punishers (which involve taking away)*
'stop threatening'	'being ignored'
'stop tutting'	'a fine'
'being left alone'	'not to go to keep fit'
'a headache goes when you take an aspirin'	'sent to bed' (i.e. deprived of being up)

A basic way of helping someone learn is systematically to reinforce his or her behaviour. Desired actions and activities are reinforced while inappropriate and undesired ones are ignored. This is something you experience yourself and do to others all the time, but not always consistently and carefully. Indeed it is easy to send confusing messages like the mother in the next cartoon.

Whatever Willy learned in this cartoon, it probably wasn't what his mother intended.

There are a number of basic rules to be followed if your partner's goal is to learn something new and you want to be an effective teacher. Your first step would have been to draw up an objective as you did in Chapter 4. Then you can consider how to proceed using the following rules. Attention to detail becomes particularly important if your partner has serious difficulty

with learning. If so you will both have to work hard and consistently for a longer period.

Rules to help learning take place

1 The reward must be something your partner wants

As we have seen, a reward for one person may not be pleasurable to another. Also we all find different things rewarding at different times. There are ways of finding out what is rewarding to a person, as we saw earlier in Chapter 3.

The best source of reinforcement is usually another person; social rewards, such as praise, a smile or a hug.

But there can be problems if the affection you offer is *not* rewarding. As Kiernan *et al.* (1978) point out: 'It is hard for any helper to persevere in offering a genuine smile or hug, if the response is continued rejection, turning or pushing away. We learn from each other.' To get around this problem, it can be necessary to pay attention, first of all, to *making yourself rewarding*. If your partner associates you with all kinds of pleasant experiences, then you yourself are likely to become rewarding. Then perhaps a smile or a hug will begin to become a genuine two-way reward.

Another form of reward in common everyday use is, of course, food, and particularly sweets. Whether used intentionally or not, all parents know how much they can influence a child's behaviour. After a while, though, sweets and hugs can lose their appeal as well as becoming rather a distraction.

Star charts have become a well-established method of offering reinforcement systematically and very easily. These involve, quite simply, offering a paper star to stick on a chart every time the appropriate behaviour has occurred. Sometimes the star becomes a reward in itself, the colourful chart being a symbol of approval and success; or sometimes when the stars add up to an agreed total a real reward is available. This could be anything from a trip out or a new comic, to something expensive and special like a new bike. Other 'token' systems can be used – collecting coupons, coins or ticks can all operate in the same way and are more age-appropriate for adults. Some ground rules have to be observed, though, or the system will almost certainly go wrong.

- As with any method, make sure the objective itself is something you both want to achieve.
- Be enthusiastic about setting up the system and make sure there is an early opportunity for putting a first star on the chart.

- Make sure it is easy to win stars to start with. Do this by setting easy targets for behaviour – not by setting hard ones and then bending the rules. For example, 'See if you can get out of bed only *once* tonight,' rather than 'Stay in bed all night!'
- Never *threaten* that stars will not be given or will be taken away. This instantly transforms the game into a punishment and it will no longer work.
- When an occasion arises, as it will, when no star can be awarded, be encouraging as well as matter of fact about it: 'Never mind, maybe tomorrow it will work out better.'

It is often surprising how well this can work. Anger and frustration can evaporate as the people enjoy what becomes a shared game.

2 The reward must be rewarding
Not only must the reward be something your partner wants, it must be important enough for him or her to notice. In the face of serious learning difficulties you may have to exaggerate the usual rewards. A pat on the head or a smile, for example, may not be enough, and an affectionate cuddle and enthusiastic words of praise may be necessary to make an impact.

On the other hand, people can sometimes be more rewarding than they realize. Offering affection to someone by cuddles and smiles can have quite profound effects on relationships which must be thought through carefully. The story of Yuris, told to us by the home tutor involved, shows how easily problems can arise.

Yuris

'Yuris was a well-built 15-year-old young man. The problems began at school. Incidents such as exposing himself to girls in the cloakroom had been reported, but that was not the main cause for concern. Over the past two or three years he had increasingly withdrawn into his own world. He would sit for hour after hour rocking back and forth and muttering to himself. He would ignore anyone who came near and if they tried to catch his eye he would look away. He was moved to a residential school, but he became violent and destructive and was removed after a couple of weeks. He was then given a home tutor, just as a short-term measure.

The educational psychologist involved, together with the home

(*continued*)

tutor, decided that the first thing that needed to happen was Yuris needed to make some contact with people. They planned a programme, therefore, which involved the home tutor, a young woman, nodding and smiling whenever she established eye contact with Yuris. The programme did work in a way. Yuris did have more eye contact, as the detailed records showed. Unfortunately he also became affectionate towards her and began to make strong sexual advances towards her.

It isn't difficult to see why, if you look from Yuris's viewpoint. He was locked into a lonely world and then suddenly there was a young woman nodding and smiling every time she caught his eye. Behaviours have meaning that go far beyond the behaviour itself. Yuris misunderstood, but so did the educational psychologist and the teacher: we cannot think about behaviour without thinking about the relationships it represents.'

3   The reward must be immediate and consistent

A reward must happen at once to make the connection quite clear. It should also be consistent and happen every time if your partner is just beginning to learn something new. As the behaviour becomes established, all being well, it will tend to bring its own reward. Michael Knight will quickly be encouraged by success on the moped itself, for example, and will only need some praise and encouragement occasionally to keep him going. On the other hand, a young child like Tracey may require careful reinforcement to learn to feed herself, but, as the process is mastered, she too will find the action of getting food to her mouth at her own pace becomes its own reward.

Punishment brings its own difficulties. Like reinforcement, frowns and disapprovals are a usual part of the flow of communication. However, the systematic use of punishment as a way of helping someone learn causes problems. For instance, it tells the learner what not to do, but does not, on its own, tell anyone what to do instead. More worryingly, it can have unwanted efects on your relationship. It is not, of course, a disaster if a parent loses his or her temper or if you show feelings of anger towards your partner. What we are saying is that punishment is not something that should be deliberately built into a scheme to help someone learn. Newson and Hipgrave (1982), in their book for parents, put it this way:

'It seems to us that it is impossible to use such methods [punishment] while still being interested in human communication!'

4 *One step at a time*

The mothers in the first cartoon (page 98) broke down the task of 'choosing yoghurt' into simple stages. This can be an essential part of helping someone with a learning difficulty to acquire a new skill. For instance, if your partner wants to be able to tie a knot in a neck-tie the task may be broken down into: (a) lift collar, (b) fasten collar button, (c) place tie round neck with wide end in right hand, narrow end in left hand . . . and so on. Whelan and Speake (1979) found 31 small steps to this task. It is important that this breaking down into small steps is tailored to the person. As a rule of thumb, each step should be small enough to be achieved within one week. Taking the above example, one person may require 31 weeks to learn to put his tie on, in which case the analysis by Whelan and Speake would be suitable. Another person may require only four weeks, in which case the whole task should be broken down into just four steps. It might even be that the objective could be achieved within a week, and the task would not need to be broken down at all.

Activity

David is a young man of 26 years who has recently moved into a group home. He would like to be able to make a pot of tea for himself and his room mate. He has tried several times, without a complete disaster but without success. He can follow instructions if they are not complicated and has a good relationship with Maureen, the home help. Maureen has agreed to help David achieve his objective. In precise terms his objective is to be able to make a pot of tea for two and have everything ready on a tray, without supervision, every morning.

Try to break the task down into four stages, which he could learn one week at a time.

STEP 1:

STEP 2:

STEP 3:

STEP 4:

There are quite a number of ways in which this task could be broken down, and David and Maureen would have to work out their own approach together. You can have a look at the two possibilities we have outlined here, and see how they compare with your own suggestions.

First possibility
STEP 1:   When the kettle boils, David will pour the water into the teapot, which already has the teabags in it, and place the teapot on the tray, which Maureen has prepared.
STEP 2:   David will load the tray with cups, saucers, spoons, milk jug and sugar bowl, and then go to Step 1.
STEP 3:   David will put the teabags in the pot, check the milk jug is half filled and the sugar bowl is half filled, and then go to Steps 2 and 1.
STEP 4:   David will fill, plug in and turn on the kettle, plus Steps 3, 2 and 1.

In this first example did you notice that David begins with the last step, and thus gets a sense of success right from the start? Maureen's involvement would be to carry out the task up to where David takes over at each step.

Second possibility
STEP 1:   David will carry out the whole task with verbal prompts, where necessary, with physical help from Maureen.
STEP 2:   David will carry out the whole task with verbal prompts, but not physical help from Maureen.
STEP 3:   David will carry out the whole task with Maureen present to give encouragement and confidence.
STEP 4:   David will carry out the whole task without supervision.

What is being 'broken down' here is the task in terms of the amount of help or supervision being given to David. We look at these aspects of learning programmes in greater detail next.

5 *Prompting*
The mothers in the cartoon helped by prompting. The most direct way to help someone learn is to *prompt* them *physically*, that is, to guide the person's hand, say, through the difficult part of the task. As usual, this is a way of helping which is something most parents do. A parent of a baby may, for instance, physically help the infant guide the bottle of milk to the mouth. With an older child, parents might hold the child's hand and toothbrush, and physically help with teeth cleaning. You may be able to use physical prompts in helping your partner learn a new skill gradually. This

can boost confidence to start with by making sure his or her attempts are successful. You can then gradually reduce the amount of help, as your partner's skill develops.

You can also prompt by pointing, giving instructions or asking questions; for example, 'Did you remember to switch the kettle on?' Take care, though, not to smother your partner with help. It is easy to get into the habit of offering too much help and guidance. Prompts should be gradually dispensed with as he or she masters the task, as in the second approach for David. Don't just stand and watch though waiting for a mistake, or you will both be on edge. Busy yourself with something else alongside, just being ready with reassurance and support if necessary.

6 *Demonstrating*

The conventional wisdom that 'actions speak louder than words' is true in many circumstances. Both children and adults learn much by copying the behaviour of others. Think, for instance, of how much easier it is to show someone how to 'make a pot of tea' than it is to explain in words. The first mother in the cartoon sequence was helping by demonstrating.

What if your partner does not seem able to copy things other people do? In their book *Starting Off*, Keirnan *et al.* (1978) make suggestions, which we have adapted here, to encourage the development of imitation of both sounds and gestures:

- Play imitation games, where you copy what your partner does, and make it a joke together.
- Start by doing things, such as clapping and making animal noises, *together* rather than you doing it first.
- Start with the simplest behaviours, with sounds and gestures your partner already knows, before introducing anything new.
- Look for increasingly accurate imitation; any sound will do to start with, but then you will want to distinguish 'da da da' from 'ma ma ma', for example.

Reinforcement, physical prompts and step-by-step approaches can all be used to help someone learn to imitate. If imitation can be established, many more possibilities can open up for them.

Play and recreation

We have been talking about encouraging individual development by the use of teaching techniques in situations where you and your partner have a specific skill-based objective in mind. In these situations, even if you have both agreed on the objective, you are essentially playing the role of teacher or helper. The relationship is still two-way, of course, but it is not equal. In relation to the teaching task you are the *leader*.

With play and recreation this situation can be reversed and you can *follow* your partner's lead. This skill may come naturally to you, or you may find it hard to acquire. It's a bit like 'person-watching', but we could call this 'person-following'. It involves attending to, responding to, and following on from whatever your partner shows an interest in. Some of the best teachers work in this way because they can then build on the children's real interest and hold their attention. They know that interest and attention are the crucial starting points for learning to occur.

The story of Peter, who learned eventually to do a bit of following, illustrates how important this can be.

Peter — learning to follow rather than lead

'Peter Dempster was a young medical student who came as a volunteer on a holiday scheme for young people with handicaps. His partner was Martin, a young man of 17 years with Down's Syndrome. Peter was keen and enthusiastic, ready to work hard for this couple of weeks and, above all, wanting to succeed with Martin. The emphasis of the two weeks was on providing opportunities for learning social skills – a chance to get out and about and practise activities like catching buses, using the phone, going to cafes, or using public toilets. Martin's programme had been worked out beforehand by the professional in charge, with his parents, and success was seen in terms of helping Martin to acquire some of these skills.

The trouble was that no one had thought of consulting Martin.

Peter's enthusiasm was dented by the end of the first day when Martin remained withdrawn and stubbornly unco-operative, rejecting Peter's every advance. On the second day, he grew even more sullen and depressed, and to Peter it seemed that all his good intentions were being rejected. Didn't Martin want to learn? Didn't he want to take advantage of Peter's kindness and these opportunities he was offering? Peter began to withdraw too.

So far, they had no common ground, no understanding of each other, no positive relationship to take them forward. The most important stage of getting to know each other somehow had not

(continued)

happened.

But then, just as everyone began to despair, the relationship began to blossom. Perhaps it was necessary for Peter to withdraw a bit, and lower his expectations before Martin could begin to play his part and assert his wishes and interests. Peter began to follow Martin's lead and they joined in some of the other activities going on around them. Although Martin had only a few single words of speech, he could show his enjoyment with a broad smile and loud laugh. Peter began to understand the things Martin enjoyed, and with the understanding came enjoyment of his company. Martin too no longer felt bewildered, and enjoyed, in his turn, the company of this new person in his life.

Together they watched a younger child working with paper and pencil. This was not a suggestion on Martin's programme. After all, surely social skills were "more important" for him, and his language was very limited. But Martin wanted to write. Martin and his volunteer made this discovery just by being together, trying things together, getting to know and trust each other's judgement. So Martin learned to write an M for Martin. Sheet after sheet was covered with large Ms – "Up and down and up and down", Peter would call, prompting him with real delight as Martin beamed with pride and covered another page.

The Ms that they produced would not change Martin's life, not help him catch a bus or use a phone, but they really mattered all the same. They mattered as a goal that he had set himself and achieved, but even more they mattered as a symbol of their relationship. They seemed to offer proof of how they had come to know and like each other.

The holiday schemes were a great success each summer and the professionals involved felt well-pleased with the achievements of the individual children. It was a parent, though, who summed up the real success of the venture: "All these young people – they've become real friends to our children. That's what matters. It shows it can happen." Being together, working together, learning to enjoy things together, had proved the basis of getting to know and like each other.'

As you did with 'person-watching' earlier, try following your partner's lead next time you have an opportunity. Follow your partner's lead in conversation, in what he or she wants to do, or in where his or her interest or attention is directed. By concentrating on your partner's interests you may find you can together open up new challenges and develop new skills and abilities. Here you will not be aiming at specific skill-based objectives. You will be thinking more in terms of process or experiential objectives as discussed in Chapter 4. Remember that earlier, in Chapter 5, you looked with your partner at circumstances and other people, and at interactions. Here your focus is on your partner's development and learning. So, in general terms, you will be hoping to expand your partner's range of experience, ability and enjoyment.

Play and *recreation* are broad terms to describe activities that people engage in for pleasure alone. They offer a means of finding out about yourself, other people and the world around you. Not only children play. Jeffree and Cheseldine (1984) show in *Let's Join In* that, whatever it is called, play is just as important at later stages of development.

Play

How can you and your partner find ways of opening up development and learning. If your partner is a child, the main thing is that he or she is 'playing', is happy and involved, and finds the toy or activity inherently rewarding. If so, then the child will be learning. Elizabeth Newson (1979) suggests four things to ask yourself with toys and activities:

1   Does this toy or game capture interest, tempt exploration or lead to any kind of involvement?
2   If the toy or activity does this, can you or the child develop this initial response in any way?
3   Does the toy, or can you, provide clear messages of success or achievement?
4   Does the toy allow the child to reach towards higher levels of achievement when he or she is ready? Does it allow for a challenge, and not simply a rehearsal of what the child can already do?

The Newsons suggest that the child will quickly lose interest if any of these four points are not met. Encouraging a child to play, then, involves finding out the child's interest and providing imaginative play materials which can be used in different ways by the child. It also involves changing activities and materials as the child's interest wanes. Jeffree *et al.* (1978) provide the following guidelines for someone wishing to encourage play:

● Play with the child's toys yourself, as an encouragement for the child to join in.
● Show pleasure in the child's play.
● 'Do not spoil the game.'

The child must play because he or she wants to.

Perhaps at this point you are thinking that this section does not apply to you. For instance, parents of a child with a learning difficulty can feel that their child simply *does not* play. It may help if you try to see it from the child's point of view, as Newson and Hipgrave (1982) suggest. Would you be bored with this toy if you had the same handicap? Is it too complicated for your child to see the point of the toy? If you can see through the child's eyes you may understand why the game is not interesting. Such insight can be the starting point for working out ways in which play *can* become both possible and rewarding.

Thinking of yourself as the child's first plaything – tickling games, peekaboo and so on – may be an appropriate starting point, before leading on to other playthings which make interesting sights and sounds.

Recreation

What about recreation for adults? In many ways the principles are the same as in 'play'. If your partner is an adult you will already have considered some leisure activities in drawing up the aims and goals together.

Activity

What makes a successful recreational activity for your partner?
Think about the activities he or she enjoys, or might enjoy, and consider what it is about the activities and the reaction to them that makes them feel successful. You could look back to the points and guidelines for play to help you because the rewards are essentially the same.

People will vary in what they want from recreation, but any of the following might be important features for your partner:

- provides interest
- feels involved
- it's fun
- a shared activity
- no fear of failure
- can try new things safely
- enjoys the company
- new skills to develop
- absence of boredom
- it's relaxing
- helps to build confidence

- a challenge available
- can join in
- feels part of it all.

Recreation offers people scope to gain what they choose. Some may focus on skills, enjoying the challenge of learning something new or stretching themselves.

'There is a vast scope in recreational activities for developing many other skills,' suggest Jeffree and Cheseldine (1984):

- fine co-ordination, as in darts or snooker
- the use of number skills, as in the simplest board game
- reading skills – from recognizing symbols to following directions
- social skills – learning to take turns, communicating with other people, and acting in a socially appropriate manner

Others may simply enjoy a shared experience which develops their self-confidence through taking part in activities like other people.

Tom McAusland (1979) says that leisure activities can help people 'to try out new ways of looking at the world'. They can help people over the stresses and strains of life, or they can be for sheer enjoyment. How far you and your partner see recreation as a personal challenge or as a means of relaxation will be your choice together. If you can help to create enjoyment and involvement then you and your partner will have found at least one way forward. Individual development is not just about acquiring new skills. It is also about personal growth, a sense of personal value and a sense of having a part to play. All of these happen through relationships with other people.

Remember the two key questions that emerged in Chapter 1:

- How *can* positive two-way relationships be encouraged, to offer opportunities for growth and well-being?
- How can communication be improved?

The approaches in this chapter, focusing on circumstances, interaction and now on individual development, all take account of this overall direction. Your particular aims and goals in your Shared Action Plan will vary, but the kind of suggestions offered here should help you and your partner to arrive at ideas which will begin to provide some answers to these questions.

Shared Action Plan activity

All the planning forms for the Shared Action Plan have, of course, been completed by this stage. The plans are now being put into action. Keeping in mind the ideas we have raised in this chapter, read again through your action planning form. Is there anything you want to change in the light of the ideas here?

There may not be any changes you want to introduce at this point, but perhaps as you move on to further stages of your action plan or develop plans with other people, you will find you can refer back to and draw on ideas from this chapter: ideas about influencing the way other people behave; ideas about acting as a mediator; and ideas about helping and encouraging individual development.

In the final chapter of this workbook we shall be talking about the importance of keeping track of where you are going, and sharing a process of review and evaluation with your partner.

CHAPTER 6
KEEPING TRACK:
REVIEW AND EVALUATION

WHY KEEP RECORDS?

What have we achieved together? What are we moving on to now? Looking back and looking forward is part of an active process of learning. It is where you begin in Chapter 1 of this workbook and it becomes the central focus again in this final chapter.

Think first about why you might keep a *written* record. Normally you do not have to write things down in order to keep track and to learn from what is happening. Learning is part of everyday contact between people. You act on your assumptions and learn from the outcome how accurate you are. Nevertheless, many people do write things down sometimes. Think for a minute how writing things down helps you.

Activity

What do you write? Below are five examples. Next to each write an example of your own.

EXAMPLES   YOUR EXAMPLES
Notes for shopping
A diary
Birthday reminders
Thank you letters
Simple poetry

Why is it helpful to write things down? Suggest a few reasons why it is useful.

YOUR REASONS

There are many kinds of reasons for writing things down. Do your reasons fit into any of these categories?

● It can help in sharing information and feelings.
● It can improve our awareness and understanding.
● It can act as a reminder, a set of instructions and a memory bank.
● It can provide encouragement and reinforcement for us.
● It can help in planning and reviewing progress.

The written forms in a Shared Action Plan can serve all these purposes. In this approach you are planning, working together and learning over long periods of time. There are also a number of people involved and the plans and strategies may be quite complex. In these circumstances it becomes essential to keep a record of what happens.

The written records become one of the greatest strengths of a system like this. They can provide open information which can be remembered, reviewed, reconsidered and revised. They can be built on, changed or abandoned, but there's always the record as a firm basis for planning the change. For the plan co-ordinators and other key people, this can be of particular value.

ACCESS

Some people with learning difficulties cannot read or write, or can only do so with difficulty. For them written information creates difficulties. Using written records at meetings, for instance, can put the individual at a disadvantage. And yet we are still suggesting that written records are important. How can this be justified?

One strong argument is that written records are to the advantage of the individual, especially if he or she can *own* them. It is even easier to baffle and distort if nothing is written down. This way there is open accountability and the possibility exists of other people acting on behalf of the individual.

Activity

If written records are valuable, despite the difficulties, are there ways of reducing the problems? If your partner cannot read, how can he or she be helped to feel it *really is his or her* Shared Action Plan?

JOT DOWN A FEW SUGGESTIONS

It was the second question that caused considerable concern for the Hawkes family. Not only is Michael a very poor reader, he has no wish to read and shows no regard for any sort of written material. They took a number of steps to overcome this problem.

- As each form came under discussion it was read out to Michael by Beth. She did this, pointing to each word as she read it so that Michael was not left out in any way.
- They kept a notebook of rough notes before filling in any of the forms. In this way everyone was able to agree exactly what had been said and what was to go on the forms before it was filled in.
- Wherever possible Michael's own words were used on the forms.
- They used photos and pictures (some drawn by Michael) on the forms.
- They made a wall-chart version of Form D so that everyone could see who was to do what and things could be ticked off as they were done.
- Their long discussions with Michael, looking at each question in many different ways, also helped, of course.

There are a number of other issues about access which arise whenever written records are kept. *Who* keeps and writes the records? *Where* are they kept and who can get at them? Are copies to be made and for *whom*? Such decisions will depend in part on confidentiality and privacy. But *who* decides that? In Shared Action Planning these decisions would be made by the key people at the outset.

Form E, Keeping Track, offers one way of keeping a record of what is achieved. Have a look at this now to see what information is asked for, and look too at the instructions for filling in the form in section 4.5 of the 'Forms and Guidelines' appendix. No one type of record-keeping, however, is likely to fulfil all requirements and in this chapter we shall be looking at several approaches which may be useful at different times and in different ways.

EXAMPLES OF RECORD KEEPING

Keeping a diary

There are *many approaches* to diary-keeping:

- A diary may be personal and private, for your own use only.
- A diary may be a shared process, where two of you agree together what to record: perhaps you and your partner in the Shared Action Plan or two care staff or parents.
- Or, it may be shared in the sense of a dialogue between people, as with a home/school diary, for example.

Diaries can also differ in their *contents*. What you choose to record is up to you. This flexibility is one of the advantages of using a diary approach. It can describe incidents, achievements, setbacks, decisions, feelings or reactions according to what seems important at the time. Diaries can also vary in how frequently they are written. They are usually thought of as daily diaries, but that is not essential.

'Julie's Diary' describes one approach to diary-keeping and what her foster parents got out of it. Diaries can serve different purposes and often these don't become clear until you try keeping a diary for yourself.

Julie's diary

'You read a short passage about Julie in Chapter 1. Something that Julie's foster parents found invaluable in caring for her was to keep notes. They called it "Julie's Diary" although Julie herself never saw it. It was written almost every night without fail when Julie had gone to bed. There was no set system to the diary. The foster parents would simply discuss everything "significant" that had happened during the day and make notes of the major points.

They saw that this diary played a very important part in their life with Julie. Often Julie's behaviour would get worse, and they would get depressed and feel that they would never make progress. At these times a look through the diary would often help them see that though things might look bad, there had been general improvements. They also found that keeping a diary helped them share and clarify their own thinking. At times it was as if they didn't know what to think

(continued)

until they had talked it over with each other and their diary. It helped them, too, to get a fuller picture of their life with Julie. Quite often one would be able to tell the other about things they had not noticed.

Finally, it helped them in communicating with others about Julie, particularly her social worker. "Julie's Diary" provided a good basis for discussing her progress (or sometimes lack of progress) with the social worker and other professionals involved.'

Activity

Try keeping a diary with your partner for a short while – maybe for the next week or two, perhaps a few minutes a day at work or at home – in a notebook for occasional thoughts. Below we suggest some advantages other people have found. You could add in anything that strikes you when you try it yourself.

Keeping a diary seems to help because it:
- improves communication and increases awareness
- acts as a reminder and memory bank
- provides encouragement
- gives a basis for planning

Some important points to remember about keeping a diary are:

- Who it belongs to is important. Sometimes it will be important for the person with a learning difficulty to feel that it is his or her diary. This did not happen with Julie. Maybe she *would* have been interested to know about it.
- A diary does *not necessarily* lead to improved communication or planning. It can, for instance, become a daily chore, done with little thought and as quickly as possible.
- A diary should not substitute for other forms of communication such as face-to-face meetings between a parent and teacher. As Julie's diary showed, it can actually serve to support such communication.

Making notes

There are many kinds of notes you might choose to make:

- Notes could help to make sense of somebody's life history, as happened for Richard. You read about him in Chapter 3 of this workbook.

- Notes could involve a kind of scrapbook about somebody, as was done for Tracey by her mother. This was a personal-life book which detailed her life through pictures, people's memories of her and factual information about her childhood.
- Notes could provide a record of a particular period of someone's life or some particular experience such as a holiday. This can help to make sense of what has happened, particularly at times of change such as moving house or when someone has died or moved away.
- Notes could be made as a record of meetings or discussions. Formal minutes are not always essential, but notes kept at self-advocacy meetings, for example, help the participants to keep track of issues they have discussed and to share decisions about where to go next. One example of this is shown in the report of the class on 'Speaking for Ourselves'.

Speaking for Ourselves

'Speaking for Ourselves is the name of a class that meets every week in London. The class learns to express their ideas, discuss them, record them and explain them to other people. John Hersov, as the teacher, has taken notes, always trying to use people's *own* words. Then at the next meeting John can read out what has been discussed by the speakers under each topic heading, using their own words. This has the positive effect of establishing a particular individual's contribution to the group. It is *their* words that are being used, which reinforces their own sense of identity, as well as encouraging the others to listen to what that person has to say. Each person has his or her own copy of the notes. So, even if some of them cannot read, the paper carried *their* words, and they can give it to others to read for them. Here are some extracts from the group's notes from the meeting on 13 November 1985. The group was discussing "Reviews":

- My review at the Centre seemed to benefit them more than me. Things seemed to go on as before, even after all the discussion.
- I didn't like people all throwing questions at you.
- I think they're good – showing you what the future holds, with jobs, etc.

(continued)

- Mine used to be every six months.
- People should be counselled *before* their review, so they know what they want to say, rather than just answer questions.
- People need to look at their files. They have a right to know what people have said about them.
- You need to get a chance to say what you want – if they are all talking about you.

That meeting ended with the group deciding on their topic for the following week: "Would the staff accept criticism?".'

If you are making notes – and you may find it is a habit you are beginning to develop after reading and working through this book – there are some points to keep in mind.

- They are most likely to be useful if you write about issues that seem important to you or your partner at the time.
- They don't have to be well-organized, or beautifully expressed, to be useful. Just a few notes can act as a reminder of important experiences, or help to explain some feelings of sadness or excitement.
- Making shared notes can be a valuable experience. If you do this, remember to record your partner's own words whenever possible, and illustrate points with drawings or photographs. Remember the drawings produced to illustrate relationships at the conference in America (p. 10).
- Keeping your notes in one place – a notebook, ring binder, or file – is probably the single most important factor!

Checklists

Checklists can act as reminders, or as guides for planning. They can also serve as indicators of progress or as a record of agreed tasks.

Checklists as guides for planning

One family drew up endless checklists to help them decide on a house move that would affect each of them differently. They listed advantages and disadvantages of moving or not moving for each member of the family – including Granny. It provided a way of taking into account and talking through all the issues before reaching a shared decision.

Checklists as reminders

These could include a list of daily jobs to be done in a group home – feed the cat, put out the milk bottles, take the tablets; or weekly tasks more difficult to remember, such as paying the rent, cleaning the toilet, putting out the rubbish. Such lists can be drawn up on a shared basis with an agreed division of responsibilities. An example of this happening can be found in the following account of Betty, Pat, Caroline, Derek and David. Ticking the tasks off as they are completed gives everyone a feeling of achievement.

Developmental checklists

Developmental checklists have been described already in Chapter 3, and provide a particular way of looking at progress and planning for a next step. Although they are designed as an aid to assessment, they often spark off ideas for what to try next as well.

Betty, Pat, Caroline, Derek and David: using a checklist

'Betty, Pat, Caroline, Derek and David live in an ordinary house in Waltham Forest. They had all lived in large institutions before moving into their "group home" which is part of the Outward Housing project. Helen is the Group Home Supervisor and lives with her husband and young son in a separate apartment at the rear of the house.

Moving into the house has brought many changes for this group of people. Betty, for instance, had lived in large institutions for over 30 years. She puts it quite simply, "You've got your own door keys. You can come in at 10 o'clock without the fear of anybody and make a cup of tea".

The crucial change seems to have been in the opportunities to have a say in the day-to-day management and running of their own home. To help them do this in an organized way they have a meeting each week to draw up the week's menu and shopping list. It took about six months to learn together how to work as a group with everyone contributing.

Derek took on the job of secretary and has developed an efficient system. In fact they are working well as a group now, and Helen has taken something of a back seat at the meetings, her main job being simply to try to answer any queries that arise. From their discussions each week emerges a checklist of jobs for the week, with a colour code system for those who cannot read. They pin this on the kitchen wall to guide and remind people, and help the smooth running of the household.'

Detailed records

Sometimes a very detailed plan is necessary to help someone acquire a new skill or learn new ways of behaving. Then it becomes essential to keep detailed records. They might cover some of the following points.

What is to be tried:
- a precise behavioural objective, stating who/will do what/under what circumstances/to what degree of success
- a breakdown of the task into stages
- the kind of help that will be given – prompting, or demonstrating, for example
- the reinforcement that will be given for success

What the outcome is
- a record of when the sessions were held
- successful attempts
- withdrawal of prompts or other help
- reinforcement given
- any changes of plan

'Learners' records' may be kept so that everyone can see the progress being made. Star charts, for example, may be used or, more discreetly for an adult, a personal folder with ticks indicating success.

Detailed records, above all, will have to be flexible and adapted to the individual circumstances. The account of Kevin's progress shows how important this can be.

Kevin's progress

'Kevin comes to stay with the Watson family for occasional weekends as part of a respite care scheme. His own family are affectionate and caring, but hard pressed by housing and financial difficulties. They have trouble coping endlessly with their very severely handicapped little boy as well as their three other children.

Kevin had developed some very difficult patterns of behaviour. He would bang his head continually on the wall, laughing at first and then crying with the pain. And he would chew his clothes. This was not just a case of biting and tearing the cuffs of jumpers, he would tear the jumper to shreds. If the jumper was removed he would start on his

(continued)

vest. If all his clothes were off, he would seize on anything – even the carpet – in desperation.

Then one weekend he came to them with his arms in splints, held out straight and stiff to prevent him from putting his clothes to his mouth. None of the professionals had been able to come up with a better solution. Dismayed, Mrs Watson decided she would try to do something about it. It had to be something simple and not too time-consuming. With four children of her own she is not exactly a lady of leisure. She started by trying to keep notes of *how often he chewed*.

She quickly found that it wasn't enough to record how often. She began to notice that he had periods when he chewed.

So *how often and how long* were the periods? Mrs Watson recorded them and tried to notice if *anything particular triggered* the chewing.

There seemed to be nothing specific, but her notes showed that the periods occurred at particular times of day, often in the evenings, and that they happened when Kevin was quite happy or "high".

From that information Mrs Watson began to plan:

- She would try to keep him occupied and distracted at times when the chewing was most likely to occur.
- She would try different kinds of activities and see which were the most effective.

In fact, the whole strategy worked so well that Kevin's chewing virtually cleared up before there was any need to distinguish the effects of different activities.

At the present time the head banging is still a problem, but Mrs Watson is keeping notes.'

EVALUATING SHARED ACTION PLANNING

Form E provides a way of keeping track, particularly in relation to a Shared Action Plan. Try completing the form. You can do it only over a period of time, perhaps entering a progress report every few weeks, in relation to different goals. It can be seen as a kind of summary of any other accounts – diaries, notes, checklists or detailed records – which may also be kept as you go along.

Once again the strength of the form lies in the relationships it depends on, as people share in the discussion of what should be recorded. What have you and your partner achieved together? What did you change and why? Where have you got to? What are you moving on to now? Who is doing it? The responsibility for keeping this form up to date would lie with the *two* people chosen as plan co-ordinators. They would have to keep in contact with each other and with others who might have taken on specific tasks, and work out what to enter on the form.

One of the plan co-ordinators may be your partner in the Shared Action Plan. If *not*, then an important part of the task is to make sure you are aware of your partner's views of the progress made.

Keeping all the forms together in a ring binder is likely to be a helpful way of managing them, as new forms will be added from time to time. This should be kept in the most accessible place for the two co-ordinators. Again, if this does not include your partner, then plans must be made to make them accessible to him or her or, if appropriate, to an advocate.

Who else has routine copies will depend on the feelings of the individual and others closely involved.

Careful thought has to be given to the advantages and disadvantages of circulating detailed information. On the whole, people who are not closely involved will not want a lot of detail and may be happy with an overall summary of the next meeting.

An overview and evaluation
– what do you think of it so far?

An evaluation of the plan itself has now to be made by your partner, possibly with somebody to help as advocate on his or her behalf. It was for your partner's benefit that the plan was devised, and this should be reflected accurately in the goals and objectives. It therefore makes good sense for your partner to be the key person to judge and comment on overall progress when the next main meeting comes around.

If this is to be taken seriously it will have to be planned for seriously. An individual cannot suddenly be expected to present his or her views coherently at a meeting. Time will have to be spent over the preceding period finding out how your partner feels about what has been happening. The purpose is to find out as clearly as possible *what your partner's experience has been*.

More conventionally, one would expect a review and evaluation to focus on reports on progress limited to specific objectives and outcomes. If questions are only asked about these, then that is all you will find out. By asking about the individual's experience, you open the doors to discovery.

Chance happenings

When you collect such information you may discover all kinds of unexpected and seemingly irrelevant things. Sometimes good things just crop up by chance and good luck. It is possible to imagine, for example, that you win a premium bond prize and can go on the holiday of a lifetime. On a smaller scale, little things like a new neighbour down the street or a series on TV that inspires some new idea can all cause positive changes that nobody planned for. These can be just as important and sometimes more important than the planned changes in the Shared Action Plan.

Sometimes chance happenings may seem to be side-tracks, and may not seem relevant to you. They may, however, seem very relevant to the individual describing them. When your partner keeps side-tracking to some other issue, perhaps the new budgie in the group home or the fact that his or

It may be disappointing to find that the budgie plays a bigger role.

her support worker's father had died, it may seem as if your partner is unable to keep his or her mind on more important matters. The important questions in your mind may be how your partner felt about the new leisure volunteer and the evening class they have attended together. Side-tracks should be attended to. It may be disappointing to find that the budgie plays a bigger role in your partner's life at the moment than your progressive ideas about community involvement, but it shouldn't be ignored. Unless we listen, we will not learn.

Sometimes people side-track when they actually want to avoid another issue; maybe there is some anxiety and they are dodging talking about the central action plan. Or it may be even simpler. Someone's mind isn't on this at the moment because for now the budgie is paramount. Side-tracks need not in the end be taken at face value, but they should not be ignored. They may provide important pointers to what really matters to the individual.

What kind of feedback do you want from your partner? The view will not be objective but it may not be any more subjective than anyone else's view. We all carry around our expectations and prejudices which influence what we judge the outcome to be. No one's judgements can be value-free.

The feedback should include feelings. It should not be too difficult to get a picture of whether the process generated by the action plan has been a source of pleasure or distress; anger or disinterest; excitement or frustration.

The feedback might also tell you something about whether the experiences seemed to lead to success or failure. Does your partner, for example, seem to feel good about the experiences resulting from the plan? Does he or she seem confident and positive about the ideas?

Feedback might tell you about what has been done. Sometimes a lot of things may have happened from the carer's or parent's point of view: many phone calls, planning meetings, and attempts to set up appointments or establish a new volunteer. But on the receiving end there may be nothing at all to show for it. It is important to know what has happened and what has been done from the perspective of your partner.

Finally, the feedback might tell you what your partner wants to happen next. Is Shared Action Planning *serving your partner's purposes* or is it just another hurdle to be set in the path? Is it welcome? And if so, what are the ideas for what comes next?

Activity

What of the staff and parents? How do you feel? Jot down quickly some of the reactions you have had in reading this account of feedback processes.

REACTIONS TO FEEDBACK PROCESS

Feedback brought a wide range of responses from people considering this approach: two made a comparison to cooking, one positive and the other frustrated.

It is a suggestion that made one reader feel angry and another feel interested.

One with enthusiastic while another was worried about it.

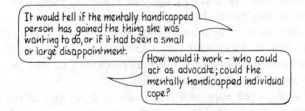

And where one felt exposed and vulnerable another felt encouraged.

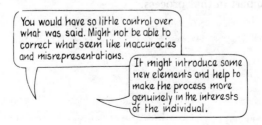

One gave both sides of the coin:

'On one level I think this is the right approach, but I confess I feel a bit wary, perhaps because for a hospital nurse this represents a reversal of the normal "who controls who" status which, whatever we like to believe, still exists. The idea that someone is going to inspect your work and possibly criticize tends to put us all on guard!'

At the same time she felt:

'As it is to help the person to live his life as he wants to, then it seems logical to let him decide if it has succeeded!'

If you are involved in Shared Action Planning and you are a key person in the life of your partner, you are likely to feel that you have a point of view too. Others who become involved, including professionals, might also want to have a say. We are not suggesting that the views of other people are unimportant. We are saying that the feedback from the individual should be seen as paramount. That *is* the evaluation. Experiences, impressions and further information can *then* be contributed from the key people and others who have been involved to clarify people's understanding of that evaluation. People will hold different views. To identify and try to understand such differences is part of the process of Shared Action Planning.

What we have done here is to suggest a change in status. If the feedback from the individual is acknowledged as the most important – however problematic it may be to obtain – then the relationship has changed. The person at the centre of the drama is put 'in charge'. It is their life and their experience, and therefore their views, that count. They may still need help, support and guidance, but your role may be to mediate their wishes as they let you know what they want out of life.

It reflects a shared approach that helps to develop a different kind of relationship – a partnership. It is a gradual process of learning for everyone. But the process itself is what counts. We hope that by making your way through this workbook, you will have been able, at least to some extent, to take part in that process.

POSTSCRIPT

MICHAEL KNIGHT AND THE HAWKES FAMILY

Some thoughts from people who
have tried Shared Action Planning

If you ask Michael Knight what he thinks of his Shared Action Plan, his answer has always been the same: 'Rubbish.' He does not like any written material. Why should he? As Peter says, 'As far as Michael is concerned it might as well be in Arabic.' There are indications, however, that even the written forms are valued by Michael. He was most indignant one evening when Peter had left the forms at work and everyone thought they were lost. What Michael has enjoyed has been the discussions he has had with Peter and Beth. He says that he doesn't like the 'stupid questions' but he does like saying what he wants to happen. Beth seems to get to the heart of the matter for them all when she says the the best thing has been simply 'time together'.

When Peter and Beth talk about what they have all gained from doing a Shared Action Plan together it is the 'spin-offs' they talk about. They feel very strongly that given time it will have 'valuable insights for Michael, helping him learn to think ahead'. They feel too that it is helping Michael to express himself. Michael says what he thinks other people want to hear. Peter and Beth feel he plays a part with a 'coy little boy routine'. Going through the Shared Action Plan is helping him to say what he really thinks, because he can see his words being written down and acted upon. They think it is helping him gain confidence in himself and in them, because he sees that they keep to their word. Quite apart from Michael, they feel they have gained a lot from spending this time together. Perhaps like other couples who both have jobs and four children they feel at times that they 'pass like ships in the night'.

Have they drawn anyone else into their Shared Action Plan? Peter and Beth have been following Michael's wishes on this question. They included an ex-teacher of Michael's in their discussions, although their preference would have been to look ahead and have someone from the ATC where Michael goes now. The teacher is a friend of the family and her role has been to help Michael by acting as his advocate. After that was accepted, Michael then felt that he *would* like someone from the ATC to be involved and they will be looking into this. As to involving other professionals, Peter and Beth think the Shared Action Plan has helped them in being able to say exactly what they want from professionals. Professionals, they say, 'can put words in people's mouths' so it helps to have thought through your goal so that then you can 'follow up your investigations using professionals'.

Michael, Peter and Beth have been learning as they go along with the Shared Action Plan approach. They have continually used and adapted it to suit their particular requirements and are continuing to do so. The main things they would say so far are:

● The person with a learning difficulty must see this as *his* or *her* Shared Action Plan.
● It takes time: 'Don't rush it.'
● Discuss the same points again and again: 'It's a matter of asking the same questions in different ways.'
● Make plenty of rough notes. Don't be in any hurry to fill in the forms. Write down people's thoughts first.
● It is better to have lots of brief sessions: 'You have to catch your moment.'

If you go back in a year's time they may have many more points to make. They are learning as they go.

APPENDIX
FORMS AND GUIDELINES

INTRODUCTORY NOTE

The appendix provides a summary of the Shared Action Planning Process, with guidelines on how to go about it, and sample forms which can be copied and re-used as necessary. The forms are free from the usual copyright restrictions for this reason. The size and design of the forms may need to be adjusted to suit the circumstances and requirements of the person with a mental handicap and the key people in his or her life.

What is Shared Action Planning?

1.1 Understanding the words
Shared
Action plans are *shared* when they start with key relationships and work outwards from that central starting point. They involve joint decisions, the pooling of ideas and working together with a person who has a mental handicap.

Action
Shared plans of *action* are about identifying what needs to be done and making sure it happens.

Planning
Shared action *planning* happens when there is co-ordination, organization and people know who is responsible for doing what.

1.2   It involves:
Aims and goals
Making decisions about the direction of change and steps to be taken along the way.

Assessment
A continuing process of discussion, shared experience, observation and negotiation with the individual concerned and with others who can contribute useful information and suggestions.

Actions and strategies
Making decisions about who is to do what, and working together to reach goals.

Review and evaluation
Sharing views about the progress that has been made, and deciding on the next stage.

Why Shared Action Planning?

2.1   A process of sharing can:
● help people with a mental handicap, together with the key people in their lives, to develop and express their wishes and goals, and to control decisions which shape their lives
● provide a way of involving others in reaching their goals
● be a means of exploring conflicts and differing interests and viewpoints

2.2   A process of action can:
● allow people with a mental handicap, working with key people in their lives, to reach their goals, in their own time, in their own way
● promote the skills, experiences and relationships involved in participating fully in the community
● expand the skills of everyone involved

2.3   A process of planning can:
● co-ordinate the efforts of everyone involved
● provide open information as a part of reviewing progress
● help ensure lines of accountability which will best safeguard the quality of services

2.4   Carrying out a shared action plan can help:
● people with a mental handicap and the key people in their lives
● to share, negotiate, participate and communicate with each other
● to relate to each other on an equal basis

How to use Shared Action Planning: general planning

3.1 The whole process should aim towards control by the person with a mental handicap (i.e. self-advocacy). When the person is unable to express his or her wishes, every effort should be made to appoint an advocate (i.e. citizen advocacy).

3.2 The first stage of planning should involve mainly the person with a mental handicap, their family, carers, or other key people in their lives.

3.3 Some broad aims should be decided early on in the planning process.

3.4 The people who attend any meetings in a Shared Action Plan should be invited by or be acceptable to the person with a mental handicap.

3.5 A Shared Action Plan is a tool which must be used in ways that suit the circumstances and requirements of the person with a mental handicap and the key people in their lives.

(a) The number of people involved can vary. The whole process may be undertaken by the person with a mental handicap and one or two key people. Sometimes more people may become directly involved, attend meetings, and share in the planning process so that services can be co-ordinated.

(b) The amount of detail in the planning can vary. It may be sufficient to clarify long-term aims. For example, a person's aims may indicate that no change and no modification in services is required. For others, very specific and detailed plans of who is to be responsible for doing what may be needed.

3.6 The forms should be completed in plain language.

3.7 Shared Action Planning does *not* just involve a set of forms. It is a process which will develop communication and supportive two-way relationships between people.

How to carry out Shared Action Planning: the forms

4.1 Form A: Background information

- The task here is to consider who should be involved in planning, advising and co-ordinating the Shared Action Plan.

- The key people will usually be those most closely involved. Three or four will probably work best. More than four would become complicated. Key people may include parents; the individual with mental handicap or an advocate on his or her behalf; and closely involved workers or volunteers. If there is already a key-worker system operating, that person could be an obvious choice. Otherwise it will

depend on what seems most appropriate according to circumstances.
- The plan co-ordinators are the two people who take on the responsibility for keeping the plan moving, making sure forms are completed, setting up meetings, etc. They share this task, not necessarily equally, and it will normally be best if they come from different bases, e.g. not two members of care staff or two parents, though this will depend upon how and where the plan gets going. Normally the two plan co-ordinators will be two of the 'key people', but this does not have to be the case. Sometimes parents, individuals and close staff members may not want the responsibility for organizing the plan, even though they would remain the key people in the plan.
- A plan consultant is suggested, recognizing that this process of Shared Action Planning may arise very informally without any professional support or input. If so, you may like to consider approaching somebody who has a wider experience, perhaps a social worker, psychologist or community nurse, to ask if he or she will offer you advice or guidance. Sometimes key workers are experienced professionals whose role involves seeing the family only occasionally, in which case they may act as plan consultant, rather than being one of the key people.
- Other contributors may make a valuable input and should not be forgotten. They will not be responsible for developing the plan, but could make helpful suggestions and comments if consulted.
- A circulation list for papers is a useful starting point and should be agreed by the key people. Is there anybody else whom you want to see copies of these forms? They may be considered to be private, which is fine, or there may be specific people you want to include or exclude. Sometimes you may want to change your minds later and include somebody else. The important thing is that the decision and control belongs to the key people.
- A description of present circumstances is also asked for on the form.

4.2   Form B: Overall aims and direction
- The purpose of Form B is to record the aims of the person with a mental handicap and key people in his or her life, and to record agreed goals.
  - (a)   *Aims* are general intentions or wishes. They answer the question, 'What would people like to see happening over the next few years?' For example, an aim might be 'to develop friendships and create leisure opportunities'.

(b) *Goals* are more specific statements of what could be achieved in the more immediate future. They answer the question, 'What would people most like to see happening over the next few months?' A goal may relate to any change or achievement, and should not always imply the need for change or progress from the person with mental handicap.

- It is recommended that this form is filled in at a meeting of the small group of key people involved.
- The process can be fairly rapid and take just one meeting, for instance when the person with a mental handicap already has clear ideas about what he or she wants to happen. It may, however, take several months for ideas to emerge and be clarified.
- Conflicts and clashes of interest should be drawn out and noted on the forms. This process itself can be reassuring and help to resolve disagreements, but, when necessary, advice would be sought from the plan consultant.
- A list of relevant questions has been provided: *Questions to think about in relation to Form B: aims and directions* (sections 5.1–5.3). These questions can be used to aid the crucial processes of discussion and negotiation.
- After filling in this form, the key people should decide whether more detailed planning is required and the advice and support of others should be sought if necessary. It may be that the clarification of aims was itself sufficient for those involved.

4.3 Form C: Positive factors and difficulties in relation to agreed goal(s)

- The purpose of this stage of the process is to gather information which will be useful in planning how the goals may be achieved.
- The number of people involved and the amount of detail recorded is determined by the plan co-ordinators.
- Information should be gathered first from the person with a mental handicap (or his or her advocate) and the other key people.
- It should refer to the *feelings, circumstances* and *abilities* of all the key people and any services/resources which seem relevant to each particular goal.
- It should be checked and amended with all the people who have contributed, and any disagreements about interpretation should be recorded on Form C.

4.4 Form D: Planning the action

- The purpose of Form D is to record the detailed planning of what is to be done by whom in order to achieve the agreed goals.

- This form should usually be filled in at a meeting of people involved in the Shared Action Plan. The number of people will vary.

  (a) It might be a meeting of 3–4 key people because they feel they do not need any further advice or support in their planning at that time.

  (b) It might be a meeting of 3–4 key people because the person with a mental handicap has made it clear he or she prefers a small meeting. Part of the planning at the meeting might be to agree who will approach and negotiate with whom after the meeting to co-ordinate the efforts of a larger group of people.

  (c) It might be a more formal occasion involving not just the key people but also service personnel. The following are guidelines for such a larger meeting of perhaps 10 people.

      (i) The plan co-ordinators should chair the meeting. If they do not wish to do so another person should be nominated by them.

      (ii) The person with a mental handicap should be present, whatever the degree of handicap, unless that person does not wish to be. Top priority must be given by everyone present to the views of the person or his or her advocate.

      (iii) The plan co-ordinators should be involved in organizing the meeting, with help if necessary, including the choice of a suitable venue and setting a reasonable time limit for the meeting.

- The first thing to do at the meeting is to review the goals in the light of the positive factors and difficulties.

- Next, take each goal in turn and decide 'What needs to happen?' to achieve the goal.

- The final discussions are to decide the first things to be done: 'Action – steps to be taken' and 'People responsible'.

  (a) 'Action – steps to be taken' are precise and clear statements of things to be done over the next few weeks. These statements are sometimes called *objectives*.

  (b) One or two people should be named as having responsibility for achieving each action.

- The plan co-ordinators should be responsible, with help if necessary, for making sure everyone who requires them has copies of the forms and for liaising between the various people involved in the Shared Action Plan.

4.5 Form E: Keeping track

- The purpose of Form E is to record answers to the questions: 'What have we achieved together?' 'What are we moving on to now?' and 'Who is doing it?'
- The plan co-ordinators should be responsible for keeping this form up to date. They will have to keep in contact with each other and with others who might have taken on specific tasks, and work out what to enter on the form.
- The plan co-ordinators should also decide when the next Shared Action Plan meeting will be held to review progress, and make any further plans thought to be necessary.
- Who is invited to the meeting will depend on the requirements and wishes of the person with a mental handicap and the other key people as described.
- The evaluation of the plan itself should be made by the person with a mental handicap, possibly with someone to act as advocate or mediator on his or her behalf.

Questions to think about in relation to Form B
– aims and directions

5.1 Living arrangements
Ask yourself:
1 How are things now?
2 How might they be?
3 How do you feel about them?

Setting and relationships
Where does this person live?
With whom?
What are the relationships like?
What is the setting like?

Comfort
Is it crowded, busy, empty?
Is it noisy, too hectic, peaceful, boring?
Are people well, healthy, happy?
Is it physically comfortable?

Responsibilities
Who does which chores, e.g. shopping, cooking, tidying?
Who makes sure this person's room, bed, etc. is okay?
Who attends to personal care, dental appointments, clothes, etc?

Time for people

How much time is there for people to do things together?

Who spends time with this person?

Who enjoys things with him or her?, e.g. chatting, making things, TV, records, cooking, giving attention.

5.2 Educational and work arrangements

Education

Where does it occur?

Who is it with?

Who are the teachers?

Is it formal or informal?

What seem to be the main aims?

How appropriate does it seem?

What does the individual want to learn?

Are there links into other opportunities, e.g. work, leisure, social contacts, further education?

Is it boring, exciting, challenging or stretching?

Who spends time with whom?

Is enough support available?

Work or work-linked opportunities

Where does it occur?

What does it involve?

Who is it with?

Is the company pleasant?

Is it enjoyable?

Is there payment?

What kind of opportunities exist for learning or advancement?

What skills are involved?

How appropriate does it seem?

Are there work-related activities?

What kind of introduction and training is involved?

Is there flexibility?

Is it boring, exciting, challenging, stretching?

Is there enough support available?

5.3 Leisure arrangements

What kind of activities?

Informal or formal?

Out or at home?

With whom?

Is access/travel easy?
Does it depend on other people?
Whose choice is it?
How much range of activity is there?
How often?
Is cost a consideration?
Are skills involved and developed?
Do learning opportunities exist?
Are the activities enjoyed?
Are there other benefits?
Are friendships involved?
Who takes the responsibility or risks involved?
Is there enough support?

Form A: Background information

_____'s SHARED ACTION PLAN   Date of birth _____   Date form completed _____

(NAME)   Address _____   Telephone No. _____

	Name	Role	Address	Tel. No.
Key people – This plan will be shared with: (*Note* Should include the key individual (and/or advocate) and people living or working in close association with him or her. No more than 3 or 4 names.)	1 2 3 4			
Plan co-ordinators: (*Note* Should be *two* people to share this responsibility, not necessarily equally. Should not come from the same base. One may be individual or parent.)	1 2			
Plan consultant: (*Note* Should be a senior member of staff who can offer advice and guidance as necessary to the plan co-ordinators.)				
Other contributors: (*Note* Should include specialists, staff, relatives or friends who can contribute but are not closely involved with the individual's day-to-day life.)	1 2 3 4		5 6 etc.	
Circulation list for papers: (*Note* Should be agreed by key people. Should normally include them, plus the other contributors listed. May include some others.)	1 2 3 4		5 6 7 8	
Present living arrangements: Where, with whom: (*Note* Should mention length and permanence of existing arrangement; any short-term arrangements, e.g. foster care, including addresses.)				
Present formal educational and work arrangements: (*Note* Should specify where, for how long and what activities are involved.)				
Present leisure activities: What, where and with whom: (*Note* Should include home-based and informal as well as outside activities.)				

Form B: Overall aims and direction

(NAME) _____'s SHARED ACTION PLAN			Date form completed _____
What would people most like to see happening over the next few years?			
(This form should be drawn up by the plan co-ordinators with the *key people* (which may include themselves) over a period of time. See guidance notes.)			
Names of key people:			
1 *In terms of living arrangements?*			
2 *In terms of educational and work arrangements?*			
3 *In terms of leisure activities?*			
Possible starting points: (goals) (*Note* Are there areas of agreement where you could identify some goals to aim at over the next six months or so? Try to find *at least one*, but *no more than three*.)	1 2 3		Explain briefly why you have focused on each goal and how it relates to overall (longer-term) aims. 1 2 3
Rejected goals			Explain reason for rejection, e.g. conflict, difficulty, non-availability of service.

Form C: Positive factors and difficulties in relation to agreed goal(s)

(NAME) _____ 's SHARED ACTION PLAN   Date form completed _____

Guidance 1   This should be completed by the plan co-ordinators on the basis of the possible goals agreed. It should provide a summary of all the relevant information gathered from key people and others, including any formal assessment results.

2   It should include reference to the *feelings, circumstances* and *abilities* of the key people and any existing services which seem relevant.

3   It should be checked and amended with all the people who have contributed and any disagreements should be recorded on the form.

Possible goal	Positive factors (including feelings, circumstances and abilities of the people involved which might help towards achieving the goal)	Difficulties (including feelings, circumstances and abilities which might get in the way of achieving the goal)
1		

N.B. After completing this form, does the possible goal still seem appropriate? Any comments can be discussed at the planning meeting and the goal modified if necessary.

Comment:

Form C: Positive factors and difficulties (Continuation sheet)

Possible goal 2	Positive factors	Difficulties

Comment:

Possible goal 3	Positive factors	Difficulties

Comment:

Form D: Planning the action (Summary form for the completion at meeting)

_____'s SHARED ACTION PLAN   Date of meeting _____

(NAME)

Overall aims(s) (Based on Form B)	Goal(s) agreed (Based on discussion of Form B and Form C and related to aim(s))	What needs to happen? (This is the main item – identify possible options, finding resources, checking on further information, drawing on advice or specialist help, clarifying cost factors, informal and formal arrangements or constraints, developing skills, using support, teaching or counselling.)	Action – steps to be taken (First steps to be undertaken to set any items in motion – details and further steps to be recorded separately.)	People responsible (With plan co-ordinators)

Form E: *Keeping track*
(To be kept by plan co-ordinators)

_____'s SHARED ACTION PLAN

(NAME)

Goal(s) (As agreed on Form D) 1	Action – steps to be taken (As on Form D) 1	Progress report Action step achieved or modified – any other comments	Date and initials	Next step (or modified goal plus next step Specify people responsible
	2			
	etc.			
2	1			
	2			
	etc.			
3	1			
	2			
	etc.			

Form E: Keeping track (Continuation sheet)

Progress report (Action step achieved or modified – any other comments)	*Date* and *initials*	*Next step (or modified goal plus next step)* Specify people responsible

REFERENCES

Argyle, M. and Henderson, M. (1985) *The Anatomy of Relationships*, Penguin Books, Harmondsworth.

Atkinson, D. and Ward, L. (1986) *A Part of the Community: Social Integration and Neighbourhood Networks,* Campaign for Mentally Handicapped People, London.

Blunden, R. (1980) *Individual Plans for Mentally Handicapped People: A Draft Procedural Guide,* Mental Handicap in Wales Applied Research Unit, Cardiff.

Blunden, R. and Revill, S. (1980) A behavioural approach, in P251 *The Handicapped Person in the Community,* Unit 5, The Open University Press, Milton Keynes.

Brennan, W.K. (1985) *Curriculum for Special Needs,* Open University Press, Milton Keynes.

Claxton, G. (1984) *Live and Learn: an Introduction to the Psychology of Growth and Change in Everyday Life*, Harper & Row, London.

Conference Proceedings on Informal Support (1985) *Personal Relationships for Persons with Developmental Disorders*, Deinstitutionalization Task Force Project, Ohio.

Cooper, D. and Hersov, J. (1986) *Self-advocacy for People with Learning Difficulties: A Staff Training Resource,* National Bureau for Handicapped Students, 336 Brixton Road, London.

Cunningham, C. and Sloper, P. (1978) *Helping your Handicapped Baby*, Souvenir Press, London.

Duck, S. and Gilmour, R. (1981–84) *Personal Relationships,* Vols 1–5, Academic Press, London.

Flynn, J. and Nitsch, K. (eds) (1980) *Normalisation, Social Integration and Community Services,* University Park Press, Baltimore, MD.

Further Education Unit (1980) Developing Social and Life Skills, Further Education Unit, London.

Humphreys, S. *et al.* (1985) Planning for Progress: A collaborative evaluation of the individual planning system in NIMROD, Research Report No. 18, Mental Handicap in Wales Applied Research Unit, Cardiff.

Jeffree, D. M. and Cheseldine, S. (1984) *Let's Join In,* Souvenir Press, London.

Jeffree, D. M., McConkey, R. and Hewson, S. (1978) *Let Me Play*, Souvenir Press, London.

Kiernan, C., Jordan, R. and Saunders, C. (1978) *Starting Off*, Souvenir Press, London.

Kiernan, C., Reid, B. and Jones, L. (1982) *Signs and Symbols: Use of Non-Vocal Communication Systems,* Heinemann Educational Books, London.

McAusland, T. (1979) *Creative Activities with Mentally Handicapped Adults and Children,* MIND, London.

McConkey, R. and McCormack, B. (1983) *Breaking Barriers: Educating People about Disability,* Souvenir Press, London.

Morris, D. (1978) *Manwatching*, Triad/Granada, London.

Murgatroyd, S. and Woolfe, R. (1982) *Coping with Crisis*, Harper & Row, London.

Newson, J. and Newson, E. (1979) *Toys and Playthings in Development and Remediation,* Allen and Unwin, London.

Newson, E. and Hipgrave, T. (1982) *Getting through to your Handicapped Child*, Cambridge University Press.

Open University (1982) *Parents and Teenagers*, Harper & Row, London.

Perlman, C. (1979) *Relationships: the Heart of Helping People*, University of Chicago Press.

Rogers, C. (1978) *Carl Rogers on Personal Power,* Constable, London.

Sang, R. and O'Brien, J. (1984) *Advocacy: the UK and American Experience*, King's Fund, London.

Sutherland, Allan T. (1981) *Disabled We Stand,* Souvenir Press, London.

Swain, J. (1977) *Spit Once for Luck*, Elek, London.

Trower, P., Bryant, B. and Argyle, M. (1978) *Social Skills and Mental Health*, Methuen, London.

Tyne, A. and O'Brien, J. (1982) *The Principle of Normalisation: A Foundation for Effective Services,* Campaign for Mentally Handicapped People, London.

Way to Go (1978) University Park Press, Baltimore, MD.

Whelan, E. and Speake, B. (1979) *Learning to Cope*, Souvenir Press, London.

Williams, P. (1978) *Attitudes and Perceptions of Others by Mentally Handicapped People,* Campaign for Mentally Handicapped People, London.

Williams, P. and Shoultz, B. (1982) *We Can Speak for Ourselves,* Souvenir Press, London.

Wilson, D. (1985) Mental handicap, in Griffiths, M. and Russell, P. (eds) *Working Together with Handicapped Children*, Souvenir Press, London.

INDEX